Endless
Income

Endless Income

50 Secrets to a Happier, Richer Life

Ted Bauman

BANYAN HILL

Banyan Hill Publishing
P.O. Box 8378
Delray Beach, FL 33482
Tel.: 866-584-4096
Email: http://banyanhill.com/contact-us
Web: http://banyanhill.com

ISBN: 978-0-692-16879-0

Notice: this publication is designed to provide accurate and authoritative information in regard to the subject matter covered. It is sold and distributed with the understanding that the authors, publisher and seller are not engaged in rendering legal, accounting or other professional advice or services. If legal or other expert assistance is required, the services of a competent professional adviser should be sought.

The information and recommendations contained in this brochure have been compiled from sources considered reliable. Employees, officers and directors of Banyan Hill do not receive fees or commissions for any recommendations of services or products in this publication. Investment and other recommendations carry inherent risks. As no investment recommendation can be guaranteed, Banyan Hill takes no responsibility for any loss or inconvenience if one chooses to accept them.

Banyan Hill advocates full compliance with applicable tax and financial reporting laws. U.S. law requires income taxes to be paid on all worldwide income wherever a U.S. person (citizen or resident alien) may live or have a residence. Each U.S. person who has a financial interest in, or signature authority over bank, securities, or other financial accounts in a foreign country that exceeds $10,000 in aggregate value, must report that fact on his or her federal income tax return, IRS form 1040. An additional report must be filed by April 15th of each year on an information return (FinCEN form 114) with the U.S. Treasury. IRS form 8938 also may be due on April 15th annually, depending on the total value of foreign assets. Willful noncompliance may result in criminal prosecution. You should consult a qualified attorney or accountant to ensure that you know, understand and comply with these and any other reporting requirements.

ACKNOWLEDGEMENTS

In quoting John Maxwell, "Teamwork makes the dream work," I would be remiss not to thank my Banyan Hill Publishing colleagues, whom without their support and effort, I would not have completed this book.

First and foremost, I'd like to thank Jocelynn Smith, Banyan Hill's senior managing editor, for her time and dedication to organizing and editing this book. Also, for ensuring it delivered the goals we set forth at the beginning of this project.

I'd also like to thank Jennifer Somerville, Tiffany D'Abate, Hillary Weiss and Alexandra Dreibelbis for their meticulous proofing and Mary Branch for her incredible design talents.

Last but not least, I thank the numerous industry gurus who shared their insights, which helped with my research.

AUTHOR BIO

Ted Bauman

Ted Bauman joined Banyan Hill Publishing in 2013. As an expat who has traveled to over 60 countries and lived in the Republic of South Africa for 25 years, Ted specializes in asset protection and international migration. He is the editor of *The Bauman Letter, Alpha Stock Alert*, and *10X Project*. Born in Washington, D.C. and raised on Maryland's Eastern Shore, Ted migrated to South Africa as a young man. He graduated from the University of Cape Town with postgraduate degrees in Economics and History.

During his 25-year career in South Africa, Ted served a variety of executive roles in the South African non-profit sector, primarily as a fund manager for low cost housing projects. During the 2000s, he worked as a consultant, researching and writing extensively on financial, housing, and urban planning issues for clients as diverse as the United Nations, the South African government, and European grant-making agencies. He also traveled extensively, largely in Africa, Asia, and Europe.

In 2008, Ted returned to the U.S., where he served as Director of International Housing Programs for Habitat for Humanity International, based in Atlanta, Georgia. During that time, he extended his travels to Latin American and the Caribbean. He continued to research and write on a variety of topics related to international development. In 2013, Ted left Habitat to work full-time as a researcher and writer. Ted has been published in a variety of international journals, including the *Journal of Microfinance, Small Enterprise Development, and Environment and Urbanization*, as well as the South African press, including the *Cape Times, New Internationalist, Cape Argus*, and *Mail and Guardian*.

TABLE OF CONTENTS

INTRODUCTION

Why do people think the way they do? Sometimes the answer is obvious. People raised in strict cultural environments often end up with similar beliefs as their parents. Those who experience profound personal dislocations are usually permanently affected.

In my case, an unusual combination of factors made me what I am. I was born into a conservative American family with strong beliefs about personal liberty and the dangers of statism. Then I ran off to Africa and experienced firsthand (a) the revolutionary overthrow of an oppressive government and (b) the rise and ultimate corruption of another.

During my years in South Africa, I developed the conviction that true freedom isn't something to be purchased. It does not result from wealth. Nor should it depend on handouts from the government.

Instead, freedom comes from a never-ending struggle by individuals and groups to define and pursue their own interests within broader society. Those interests consider the interests of others. They are not exclusive or oppressive. Freedom means coordinating with others for everyone's best interest.

But freedom never comes from politicians — at least, not from them alone. Voting will never secure freedom. Voting is important. So is speaking your mind to influence others. But freedom also requires a willingness to take direct personal action.

The strategies in this book are examples of that kind of personal action. In every case, I identify a solution to a problem, or an opportunity. These strategies are legal. But they are often buried deep in bureaucratic regulations or case law. Sometimes they are even deliberately obscured by those who stand to benefit financially or politically if you don't know about them. Other times people ignore them because they assume they are only for the rich and powerful.

Creating an asset protection trust in the state of Nevada, for example, is an inexpensive and powerful way to ensure that your assets — no matter how large or small — are protected from legal challenges. I don't mean that you can get away with crime; I mean that if you are sued, or faced with a difficult divorce, or a business partnership goes sour, whatever you vest in the trust is safe.

Similarly, the tax optimization strategies I discuss aren't illegal. Nor are they unethical. But they are often restricted to wealthy clients of wealthy tax attorneys because those attorneys like to pretend that they are difficult to implement. They aren't, and I show you how to do it.

Opportunities like self-directed individual retirement arrangements (IRAs) are little-known because the retirement-saving industry vastly prefers it that way. They tell scary stories about what can happen if you do something wrong with your IRA, then take your money and invest it in weakly performing stocks and charge you high fees. It's true IRA mistakes can be costly, but I tell you how to avoid them — without charging you an arm and a leg.

These three examples have something in common: People are often afraid to try them. They think they will get into trouble, or that they are too expensive, or too complex and risky.

That illustrates another thing about freedom: It means overcoming those fears. The best way to do that is to consult someone who truly cares about you and your prosperity. Someone who does what he does not just for a job, but as a personal mission.

I'm that someone. I know you will benefit from this book, and from the strategies for freedom and prosperity contained in it. And you should know that when you do, I will be very happy indeed!

Kind regards,

Ted Bauman
Editor, *The Bauman Letter*

INVESTMENT

T he freewheeling '80s churned out a bevy of movies about how a little guy with grit, intelligence, and a little cash could make it rich investing on Wall Street. But there's far more to smart investing than just scooping up the hottest names trading at the moment. In this section, you'll learn about several types of assets that pay out a steady stream of income, how to get paid by your country treasury, and a critical way to slash through fees that are eating away at your returns. Punch your ticket now to beating Wall Street with its own tricks.

INCOME SECRET NO. 1:

Become a "Lazy Landlord" and Collect Rent Without Buying or Managing a Single Piece of Real Estate

Wouldn't it be nice to invest in real estate and derive a steady income without having to lift a finger and actually manage the property?

Well, you can — and you don't need to put up millions of dollars of your own money to do it. The trick is to use crowdfunding sites to invest in real estate investment trusts (REITs) and, in the process, generate a substantial amount of income.

A REIT is a company that owns, and often operates, income-producing real estate. There are many types of commercial real estate owned by REITs including office and apartment buildings, hotels, hospitals, shopping centers, warehouses — even timberlands. Other REITs are focused on financing real estate.

When REITs were first created by an act of Congress in 1960, they were intended to provide a real estate investment structure similar to that of mutual funds. Today, REITs are publicly traded on the major exchanges, either public but non-listed or private. As such, there are two main types of REITs — equity REITs (which invest and own properties) and mortgage REITs (which invest in property mortgages).

Savvy investors consider REITS strong income vehicles because they generally must pay out an amount that is equal to at least 90% of their taxable income in the form of dividends to their shareholders.

However, if you were to invest in a stock market REIT, your annualized yield would average just 2% to 3%. Whereas, if you use crowdfunding sites such as FundRise.com or RealtyMogul.com to invest in REITs and real estate directly, your annualized yield could be as high as 11%.

There are other advantages to real estate crowdfunding. For one thing, they provide you with the ability to individually select the properties *you* wish to invest in. That way, you can be more selective on a project-by-project basis and build yourself a custom portfolio that is to your specific investment objectives.

In addition, real estate crowdfunding affords you the opportunity to invest in certain real estate markets that were previously off limits, such as commercial real estate.

Plus, crowdfunding doesn't require a large minimum investment. You can own a stake in a major real estate project without having to invest a large amount of money. Being able to invest small amounts of money in real estate deals, you can diversify your ownership in multiple properties. That allows you to build a more diversified portfolio with minimized risk exposure. For example, instead of investing $250,000 in one property, you can invest $50,000 in five different projects.

Another important consideration: Investments in real estate crowdfunding campaigns are not publicly traded. Therefore, they are not subject to mark-to-market valuations from minute to minute. This means the value of your real estate crowdfunded investments doesn't fluctuate. Unlike the stock price of a REIT, which can be influenced by external factors and move up and down significantly throughout each trading day, crowdfunded REIT investments provide a safe haven from market volatility.

To further explore this opportunity to become a "lazy landlord" while boosting your income, here are five of the top crowdfunding sites worth looking into:

- Fundrise
  (https://investorjunkie.com/44325/fundrise-review)
- LendingHome
  (https://investorjunkie.com/48088/lendinghome-review)
- Patch of Land
  (https://investorjunkie.com/47907/patch-land-review)
- Realty Mogul
  (https://investorjunkie.com/45797/realthy-mogul-review)
- RealtyShares
  (https://investorjunkie.com/44852/realtyshares-review)

INCOME SECRET NO. 2:

'The One Asset Class Paying Out
a Steady Income Stream

Retirement is supposed to be a time of leisure and relaxation. It's supposed to be a worry-free time where you travel, learn new things, enjoy hobbies and spend time with loved ones.

But thanks to years of ultra-low interest rates, retirement has become a frantic search for income to make all those dreams a reality.

Over the past three decades, the investment environment has changed — and not for the better — when it comes to those on a fixed income.

Interest rates have fallen sharply due to economic weakness and turmoil. The Federal Reserve has kept rates at bargain-basement levels year after year in an attempt to keep the market alive, while leaving those dependent on income out in the cold.

You may have forgotten exactly how far we've fallen.

In September 1981, the 10-year government bond yielded an average 15.32%.

By September 1990, the yield was down to 8.89%.

In September 2000, it was at 5.80%.

And today … the 10-year bond yields a mere 2.98%. That's after the Federal Reserve has gone through several rounds of rate hikes!

If you had invested $100,000 at a yield of 15.32%, you would have earned $15,320 in a year. That was more than the median annual salary of $11,669 in 1981 and would have made for a nice retirement.

Today, $100,000 invested at a yield of 2.98% gets only $2,840 per year. That is a frightening prospect for retirement income.

However, you can still find much higher yields — yields that are closer to what we saw in 2000, 1990 ... and even 1981.

These assets are master limited partnerships (MLPs), and they are different from the stocks that you've likely already traded in your brokerage accounts and 401(k)s.

In fact, there are 568 agencies slated to pay $34.6 billion over the next year to any American taxpayer with a claim on the cash.

MLPs are safe, and they are outperforming the market.

MLPs are based on the belief that if the United States of America is to remain a free nation, it needs to be self-sufficient.

However, most Americans have no idea we send over $535 billion every year to foreign countries for natural resources such as oil, metals and agriculture.

And the worst part of this policy is that most of the foreign countries receiving our billions of dollars are not only hostile to the United States, but they actively support terrorist enemies with our own cash.

But it doesn't have to be this way.

According to a prominent geological survey, there is $128 trillion worth of physical assets within the borders of the United States. These are massive resources — from oil and natural gas to core metals (think steel and aluminum) ... to precious metals like gold and silver.

That's enough money to pay off our $21 trillion national debt six times over. Or fund Social Security for the next 150 years.

Every president from Nixon to Trump has been striving to make the U.S. truly self-sufficient. Which means our country has been fighting this battle for independence for over 40 years ... yet we've continued to send $535 billion every year to foreign countries.

That's why this opportunity is so critical. And after four decades of struggling, we may have finally found the solution...

It's known as Statute 26.

It basically says that a company can operate tax-free if it becomes a designated agency.

To meet the requirements, a company must:

- Generate 90% of its revenue from the production, processing, storage and transportation of the $128 trillion of natural resources in the U.S.

- And pay out lucrative freedom checks to all shareholders.

Obviously, operating anything tax-free is a huge incentive … especially with a corporate tax rate of nearly 40%.

It's no wonder companies jumped at the opportunity to become one of these designated agencies. They would much rather pay billions of dollars to their shareholders than pay even more money to Uncle Sam.

Yet, of the 16,000 publicly traded companies that qualified, only 568 have met the guidelines to become a designated agency.

Over the next year, these agencies are set to cut $34.6 billion in freedom checks. And all you have to do is buy shares, or "units," in one of these 568 designated companies and then collect the payouts. You can get started with an investment of $10 or less, since shares of these MLPs trade like every other company on the stock market.

You can trade MLPs on major exchanges. You can purchase them just as easily as shares of a company or an exchange-traded fund. That makes investing in an MLP very easy.

When it comes to an MLP, instead of shares of a company, you are typically buying "units" of an MLP.

Instead of a being a shareholder, you're a "unitholder" of an MLP.

And where a company pays you a dividend, an MLP pays a "distribution." Just a small change in language, but the concept is similar.

The key difference comes in the treatment of their payouts to investors.

As an MLP investor, you have to pay taxes on 10% to 20% of the cash you collect. Taxes on the remaining 80% to 90% are deferred until you sell your units.

With an MLP, every time you receive a check, a portion of your initial investment is returned to you. As a result, the IRS does not consider these MLP payments as "taxable income," but rather a "return of capital." The IRS doesn't tax most of your quarterly income checks until you sell your units.

This sounds complicated, but it's really not.

Ordinary dividends must be filed on Form 1099-DIV (https://www.irs.gov/pub/irs-pdf/f1099div.pdf). Distributions from an MLP must be filed on Form K-1 (https://www.irs.gov/pub/irs-pdf/f1065sk1.pdf). This means that your taxes are going to require a little more time for preparation, but the upside is that the payments you receive for investing in MLPs should more than make up for the added tax headache.

How much more? Let's take a look at what the market has to offer right now and how we can beat it with not only great-yielding MLPs, but also units that are set to rise in value over time.

Right now, the S&P 500 Index has a pathetic yield of just 1.93%. Utilities, which have long been seen as the go-to for income, are paying out an average of 3.31%. Real estate investment trusts (REITs) aren't doing much better with an average yield of 3.85%.

And as I mentioned earlier, the U.S. 10-year note is yielding only 2.98%.

So far, we're still lagging behind even the average yield of the 10-year bond in the early 2000s.

We can do better.

The average yield of 128 high-yield, tax-advantaged MLPs is 8.9%. That matches Treasury yields we haven't seen since 1990!

Check into adding MLPs to your trading portfolio and start earning a steady stream of income.

INCOME SECRET NO. 3:

Triple Your Dividend Income With a Few Nearly Forgotten "High-Class" Stocks

So ... how much is that "hot" new common stock paying you in dividends on a quarterly basis? Two percent? One percent?

How about *0%* — because it doesn't even offer its shareholders a dividend?

Maybe it's time to start investing in preferred stock shares. They offer dividends of 6% to 7% on average.

Not only that, but they're safer than common shares of stock, which is another reason they're popular among retirees who want to boost or stabilize their cash flow.

What's the difference between a preferred stock and a common stock since both have the potential to appreciate in price?

A preferred stock is a class of ownership in a corporation that has a higher claim on its assets and earnings than a common stock. Generally, preferred stocks have a dividend that must be paid out before dividends to common stock shareholders. They also yield more than common stocks and can be paid on a monthly (or quarterly) basis. These dividends can be fixed or set in terms of a benchmark interest rate.

The finer details of each preferred stock depend on the type of share. For example, adjustable-rate shares specify certain factors that influence their dividend yield, while participating shares can pay additional dividends that are determined by the company's profits.

Preferred stocks are also classified as either perpetual or callable. Perpetual shares have no stated maturity date, while those with a call date may be redeemed by the authorizing company at a future date. Those are considered a risk and thereby generally pay a slightly higher yield than perpetual shares.

In addition to the income they generate, "called" preferred stocks provide the opportunity for capital appreciation. The risk, however, is that they will eventually be called, at which point the investor will have to replace the yield and expected income with another holding.

Since preferred stocks with a call date may be redeemed at face value (usually $25), it can be advantageous to pay as close to par value as possible (also generally $25).

Dividends from preferred stocks are usually labeled as either cumulative or noncumulative. Cumulative dividends are those that must be paid by the company (or at least accrued until the company can pay), whereas noncumulative dividends can be withheld from shareholders based on the company's profitability. That being the case, you may think it best to consider only cumulative dividends. However, they aren't as popular as noncumulative versions, so in order to truly diversify your portfolio, you may want to incorporate both.

One caveat: Preferred yields can rise into double digits or languish on the lower end of the scale. While that makes preferred stocks with higher yields more desirable, they usually come with far more risk in terms of the company's credit rating, corporate fundamentals, tax eligibility, industry market conditions and bid-ask price.

Therefore, it would be wise to balance yields with these factors when considering which preferred stocks to choose. For example, a corporate credit rating dictates the rate at which a company can borrow. So you may want to consider investment-grade companies that carry ratings of AAA, AA, A or BBB. They may pay lower rates than those rated BB or lower, but what you sacrifice in a lower yield, you'll gain in added investment safety.

Two helpful sites to broaden your understanding of the benefits of using preferred stocks to boost your retirement income are QuantumOnline.com and PreferredStockChannel.com.

INCOME SECRET NO. 4:

Get Paid $2,500 a Month From Your County Treasury

There's tax-free income hiding in plain sight.

Nearly every town across America offers it.

Multimillionaires collect it whenever they can. But most working-class families still haven't taken advantage of it.

In case you haven't guessed, I'm talking about **municipal bonds**. The interest you receive from them is exempt from federal tax.

But that's not all. If you live in the state in which they're issued, they're also exempt from state and local tax.

Plus, the tax exemption prevents the income you earn from boosting you up into a higher tax bracket ... which is one of the reasons millionaires absolutely love their munis.

Yet most middle-class investors overlook municipal bonds and, in doing so, are missing out on a great opportunity to generate additional income.

For example: $500,000 in savings placed into a tax-free municipal bond that yields 6% would generate $30,000 per year ... which amounts to $2,500 per month in interest income.

Not bad, eh? And having the benefit of being exempt from state income tax in addition to being exempt from paying federal taxes *increases* the taxable-equivalent yield. That's why the higher a state's income tax, the more likely state residents will buy their state's bonds, while states without an income tax are forced to offer higher yields to attract both in-state and out-of-state buyers.

Those states that have no income tax include: Alaska, Florida, Nevada, South Dakota, Texas, Washington and Wyoming. As such, they offer slightly higher yields to offset the fact that their bonds offer no local tax benefit to their own citizens.

Elsewhere, the rules vary. For example, New York State's municipal bonds are exempt from city and state income taxes. So, interest from municipal bonds issued in New York may be *triple tax-exempt* from city, state and federal income taxes.

Meanwhile, Utah doesn't tax its own bonds ... but it also doesn't tax bonds issued in states that don't tax Utah bonds. To put it another way, if a particular state doesn't collect taxes on Utah's bonds, Utah doesn't collect interest on that state's bonds. So, Utah residents are free to buy bonds from states with no income taxes such as Texas, Florida or Washington and avoid paying Utah state income taxes on the interest.

Among the states that tax in-state bonds are Oklahoma, Utah, Iowa, Wisconsin and Illinois.

For most other states, only interest from bonds issued within the state is exempt from that state's income taxes. So, if you invest in bonds from other states, it's likely that you'll have to pay tax on the interest from those bonds.

And what about residents of Washington, D.C.? The district doesn't tax in-state or out-of-state municipal bonds, so they can buy bonds from anywhere and not pay state or district income taxes on the interest.

Regardless of whether or not your state taxes the interest on municipal bonds, most of your tax savings are going to come from not having to pay federal income taxes. So, when it comes to dealing with state taxation, the best strategy is to diversify your municipal bond portfolio across multiple states.

INCOME SECRET NO. 5:

Supercharge Your Savings With Accounts That Pay You *25 Times* More Interest

As we all know, standard savings accounts have been offering paltry interest rates for some time now. And by paltry, I mean next to nothing. In fact, the current national average is a measly 0.08%.

But that doesn't mean you can't generate extra income from savings accounts or that you should scratch them off your list of investment options. It just means you need to find the right kind of savings account available at some of the most reputable and recognized banks in the nation.

Here's why: High yield online savings accounts from banks such as Barclays, CIT, Goldman Sachs, Synchrony and many more offer up to 2% APY versus the national average of 0.08% for standard savings accounts.

Do the math: 2% divided by 0.08% equals 25. So that's as much as *25 times more* in interest you could be accumulating with an online savings account.

Plus, besides offering much higher interest rates than the average savings account, the best of these online banks offers other perks, such as a no minimum balance, ATM access and/or free checking.

Here is just a small sampling of some of the highest-yielding online savings accounts (Note: rates can fluctuate, so check the individual bank websites for the latest APYs):

- Synchrony Bank — This one offers 1.85% APY with no minimum balance, no monthly fee and it'll even throw in an ATM card. While most internet-only banks require electronic funds transfer that can take a few days, having ATM access means quicker access to your money.

- Marcus By Goldman Sachs USA — Along with a 1.80% APY, this account requires no minimum balance, and there are no transaction fees. You can deposit funds by check or by electronic or wire transfer, and access funds via electronic or wire transfer.

- American Express National Bank — With a personal savings account, you can earn a variable 1.75% APY with no minimum balance and without any fees. Plus, the FDIC insures your deposits up to $250,000.

- Barclays Bank — With more than 300 years of history, Barclays is as dependable a bank as they come. It offers a 1.85% APY for its online saving account with no minimum balance or monthly fees.

- Ally Bank — Not only does Ally offer a 1.80% APY with no minimum balance required, but you can get a free checking account with no minimum balance that provides easy access to your funds.

- CIT Bank — It'll cost you $100 to open this online savings account, but it comes with a 1.55% APY and interest compounds daily. In addition, there are no monthly maintenance fees.

- Popular Direct — You'll need a minimum of $5,000 to open this account and you'll have to maintain a $500 balance to avoid a $4 monthly service fee, but that's because it pays a whopping (by today's standards) 2.00% APY that, over time, could generate the most interest income of comparable online savings accounts.

Just about anyone can open an online savings account and rake in hundreds, if not thousands of more dollars each year in interest compared to your average neighborhood savings bank. Which, frankly, is why I'm amazed that more retirees aren't taking advantage them.

And with the Federal Reserve on course to continue raising interest rates in the months ahead, the rates these online banks offer could get sweeter.

To keep abreast of the best offers (which are subject to change on a monthly basis), type "Best Online Savings Accounts" in your search engine.

INCOME SECRET NO. 6:

Ramp up Your Retirement Fund With This Surprisingly Simple Move

Many of us dream of retiring early — say, at 50 years old instead of 65. But all too often, it's just that — a wishful fantasy — because we simply don't have the savings or retirement income needed to sustain us for the next 20, 30 or 40 years.

Nevertheless, when William was just 38, and his wife Nancy was just 33, they did just that: They retired.

No, they weren't high-powered CEOs raking in seven-figure salaries. And they didn't win the lottery. They were your ordinary middle-class couple living in Seattle, Washington.

And yet, thanks in large part to a surprisingly simple move, William and Nancy turned a modest nest egg into a $1 million fortune ... and are on track to make $3 million in investments over the next 30 years while millions of other Americans are still struggling just to get by.

What's their "secret"?

Three words: low-cost income funds. They saved as much as they could and focused on investing in low-cost income funds rather than ordinary mutual funds. Today, 100% of their savings are in these funds because of what William read from billionaire investor Warren Buffett and Jack Bogle, founder of the Vanguard Group, on low-fee and diversification benefits.

In fact, William and Nancy invested the bulk of Nancy's money in one simple exchange-traded fund (ETF) — the Vanguard S&P 500 Index Fund. And in 2015, she made $172,500 in interest and dividend income. Basically, investing in no-cost or low-cost ETFs allows you to slash your fees from an average 4.25% to 0.25%, which makes a huge difference in your total return on investment when you factor in reinvested dividends.

An exchange-traded fund is a marketable security that tracks an index, a commodity, bonds or a basket of assets. Unlike mutual funds, an ETF trades like a common stock on a stock exchange and experiences price changes throughout the day as it's bought and sold.

The Vanguard S&P 500 Index tracks the S&P 500 and is a low-cost fund started by Jack Bogle in the 1970s. As you can see in the chart below, the Vanguard S&P 500 Index Fund has returned over 200% over the last eight years.

**Vanguard 500 Index Investor
Total Return Price % Change**

SOURCE: Bloomberg

With returns like that, combined with low maintenance fees, it's easy to see how William and Nancy were able to amass their fortune and watch it grow, enabling them to retire at an age when others are just starting to take retirement saving seriously.

Warren Buffett is such a true believer in the power of investing in low-cost ETFs like the Vanguard S&P 500 Index Fund that his estate plan specifies that if his wife outlives him, 90% of her inheritance should be put into the same ETF.

It's amazing to think that earning an extra $172,500 per year while you just sit back and watch your investment income soar could be so effortless. Yet you too can ramp up your retirement fund with this unusual "hands-off" approach to automatic income and possibly retire happily ever after much sooner than you originally planned.

INCOME SECRET NO. 7:

Increase Your Brokerage Statement $3,120 Each Year by Firing Your "Robo" Stock Adviser

Welcome to the "robo" age — complete with robocars, robocalls, robochefs, roboworkers and … yes, robo stock advisers.

What, you may ask, is a robo stock adviser? It's an automated electronic system that provides financial advice or investment management online with little human intervention. A robo-adviser provides digital financial advice that is based on algorithms executed with software that automatically allocates, manages and optimizes your assets.

These automated advisers have soared in popularity in recent years mostly because they make investing easier. In fact, there are well over 100 robo-advisery services that have the capability to allocate your assets in many different investment products such as stocks, bonds, commodities, futures and real estate. The funds are often directed toward exchange-traded fund (ETF) portfolios, and you can choose between offerings with active management styles or passive asset allocation techniques.

Of course, as we all know, there's no such thing as a free lunch … or a free robo-adviser. While they do offer competitively low fees compared to human, professionally managed investment assistance, robo-advisers like Asset Builder, Betterment, Wealthfront and others can charge up to 0.50% in their fees alone.

That may seem fairly reasonable, but you could save as much as $3,120 per year simply by ditching your robo-adviser and instead putting your money into low-fee stock and bond index funds — much like robo-advisers often do anyway.

Here's an example furnished by self-made millionaire and wealth management adviser Chris Reining…

Let's say you sign up with a robo-advisery service, deposit $3,000 in the account and set up an additional $300 investment every month. Assuming you earn an annual return of 10%, your investment would be worth $70,893.

However … don't forget there's a fee to have the service invest your money in an index fund. Let's say it's only 0.25%. You need to subtract that fee from the return to calculate what you're actually making. So now it's 9.75%. At that rate of return, your investments are worth $69,825 — so, you've already lost about $1,000 in fees. But it doesn't stop there.

Keep in mind that the robo-advisery service isn't paying the index funds fees for you. So, you have to pay those as well to the average tune of 0.16%. That boosts the total fees to 0.41% and lowers your return to 9.59%. Now your investment is worth $69,150.

No big deal? Then, consider this:

Let's say your goal is to save $1 million in order to generate $40,000 in passive income every year. You realize that to reach that goal you would have to invest a lot more money. So you start out investing the same $3,000; only now you're investing an additional $3,000 every month.

Following that strategy, you're going to end up with $1.2 million within 15 years. But how much will you pay your robo-adviser in total fees on that $1.2 million? The answer is $3,720 per year.

Now, had you invested your $1.2 million directly with the stock index fund with a fee of 0.04% and a bond index fund with a fee of 0.05%, the index fund would only be skimming off about $600 per year, putting the extra $3,120 in *your* pocket.

If you're living on $40,000 a year, can you really afford to pay an additional $3,120 (7.8% of your passive income) in fees?

It simply comes down to this: While robo-advisers charge lower fees than most financial advisers, they charge higher fees than if you simply invest in an index fund yourself. And over time, those fees can make a huge difference in your nest egg.

INCOME SECRET NO. 8:

Become an Early Investor ... With as Little as $500 ... With Peer-to-Peer Lending

Maybe you've always wanted to invest in a startup company or a venture capital opportunity, but that brass ring always seemed to be just out of reach because you simply didn't have enough funds to take the plunge ... or the amount needed was too much to finance on a credit card ... or the amount was too low for banks and angel investors to get the return they wanted.

But now anyone can become an early investor ... with as little as $500 ... and collect a steady stream of income every month.

The key is peer-to-peer (P2P) lending. It's a method of debt financing that enables you to borrow (or lend) money without using an official financial institution as an intermediary.

In other words, it removes the middleman. It's a form of crowdfunding that involves borrowing money from your peers, including other businesspeople and investors who are interested in relatively small financing amounts.

Peer-to-peer lending offers several benefits:

- No collateral is required.
- Lower interest rates are available, depending on your credit score, loan amount and loan term.
- You can repay the loan early without prepayment penalties.
- Faster approval.
- No paperwork besides a few online forms and a digital signature.

Also, you can continue using your P2P lending connection to tap additional funds once you borrow and repay the initial loan.

You can obtain P2P through sites such as LendingClub.com and Prosper.com.

Launched in 2006, Prosper was the first P2P lending company, followed in 2007 by LendingClub, which became the world's largest P2P lending platform.

Today, these are the two preeminent choices for peer-to-peer investors. Both offer good deals for early investors, but have different conditions.

Here's a comparison:

	LendingClub	Prosper
Promotions	Get up to 100,000 United Miles when investing	None
Fees	1%/year	1%/year
Minimum Deposit	$1,000	$25
Loan Term	3 or 5 years	3 or 5 years
Loan Amount	$1k-$40k consumer, $5k-50k auto, $5k-$500k business	$2k-$35k consumer
Accredited Investor	No (unless in Kentucky)	No
Note Types	Unsecured Consumer Debt, Auto Refinancing and Business Loans	Unsecured Consumer Debt
IRA Account	Yes	Yes
Source: Investorjunkie.com		

The first thing you need to do before becoming a P2P investor is find out whether peer-to-peer lending is available in your state. Although LendingClub and Prosper are regulated by the Securities and Exchange Commission (SEC), they are still subject to the laws of individual states regarding the solicitation of investors.

Currently, LendingClub is available to new investors in all U.S. states and the District of Columbia with the exception of Alaska, New Mexico, North Carolina, Ohio and Pennsylvania.

However, the LendingClub trading platform FOLIOFN — where investors trade in existing loans — is available to investors in each of these states except Ohio.

Prosper is currently available for new investors in most states, including D.C., with the exception of Alabama, Arizona, Arkansas, Iowa, Kansas, Kentucky, Maryland, Massachusetts, Nebraska, New Jersey, New Mexico, North Carolina, North Dakota, Ohio, Oklahoma, Pennsylvania and Vermont. However, it doesn't allow any additional states on its trading platform.

In terms of interest charged to borrowers, LendingClub offers an annual percentage rate, or APR, ranging from about 6% to 28% based on factors such as the borrower's FICO score, number of recent credit inquiries, length of credit history, total number of open credit accounts and revolving credit. Most borrowers tend to pay a higher interest rate for higher loan amounts and for 60-month loan terms versus 36 months.

Prosper offers slightly higher rates ranging from 6% to 34%, but also allows borrowers with lower credit scores on their platform. These rates change regularly, so be sure to check with both sites.

For more information on P2P lending offered by these and other companies, visit https://www.goodfinancialcents.com/peer-to-peer-lending.

INCOME SECRET NO. 9:

Turn Your Hobby Into a Secret
Income Gold Mine

Using the collectibles market to increase your fortune means honing in on some of your hobbies or special interests and putting your unique knowledge to work. If you love baseball, you'll have fun gathering old trading cards. If you're a comic collector, then I'll bet the idea of hunting down a rare variant cover of your favorite issue appeals to you. The same goes for coin collectors, watch enthusiasts, art lovers, wine connoisseurs, fans of rare manuscripts and so on. And no matter what, you have the thrill of the hunt — all while using an investment strategy that's proven to be exceedingly profitable for those who know how to search for the right collectibles.

Historical price charts for collectibles tend to show a very similar pattern. Be it coins, comic books or rare wines, collectibles have a history of outperforming traditional assets over time. And they tend to do so with far less volatility or correlation to traditional investment assets.

It's only logical when you consider that collectibles tend to be held in "strong hands," meaning they're largely owned by aficionados who rarely part with their collections just because of economic tribulations. That gives them stability and provides a certain counterbalance to an investment portfolio.

Of course, that doesn't mean collectibles won't fall in value; they can and do at times. But if you're investing in the long haul with the idea that you will sell a collection at auction one day — to supplement retirement or maybe pay for a kid's college education — then the growing demand for certain areas of the collectibles world means that key items will likely retain their value or grow in value over time.

These assets are a "quiet wealth" for a reason: They can help you keep some of your wealth out of the government's hands. Various organizations and Western governments around the world these days are talking about a "wealth tax" — let's call it what it truly is: wealth confiscation — as the last, best way to extinguish what is now an unmanageable debt load that our elected leaders have accumulated for us. If we ever reach the point where America imposes such a tax, the hit men in the IRS aren't likely to include hard-to-value, non-financial assets in their calculations. Collectibles, then, would be a perfectly legitimate and legal means of shielding your assets from a government that is increasingly desperate for money. It's a store of wealth that potentially has a government buffer built around it.

And collectibles — true collectibles that can't be mass-produced — hold value over time because of the nostalgia factor. Sometimes they even become a part of pop culture. Collectors want to hold on to their conquests and are willing to pay big money for them.

And that means huge profit potential.

For example, the Codex Leicester, a compilation of scientific writings by Leonardo da Vinci, was purchased in 1980 for $5,148,000, and it sold for about $30 million just 14 years later. The profit-gain increased by 443.90%, or 31.7% per annum.

Another recent example is the Fender Stratocaster guitar. One went on sale for a whopping quarter of a million dollars. It originally listed for about $250, so that's a 10,000% appreciation.

Not bad!

Nice profits aren't that rare, either. In fact, collectibles have a habit of outperforming other, more common investing avenues. In December 2014, CNBC reported that, overall, investing in high-end collectibles has been more lucrative than investing in stocks. Over the past 10 years, the Knight Frank Luxury Index (which tracks collectibles from cars and art to stamps, wine, coins and furniture) was up 182% while Dow Jones was only up 62%.

This is one investment avenue that is too often overlooked by investors and I want to give you some key tips to get started.

8 Beginner Tips for Making Money in Collectibles

Each collectible category demands a unique approach for making the most of your investment. But no matter if you're investing in wine, coins or comics, there are commonalities to keep in mind. Because the basic strategy is always the same: You need to buy the right item at the right time, preserve it well and sell it at the right moment to the right buyer.

It's deceptively simple. See, although the strategy seems like common sense, it takes an intimate knowledge of the market to execute correctly. If you don't have a healthy knowledge, it becomes extremely difficult to successfully invest money in collectibles.

Just consider the wide range of questions you have to answer: How do you begin your search? What trends are peaking? Which dealer is the perfect candidate to rate your item? What's the best way to keep your collectible in tip-top shape? What auction house should you use — if you use any?

To get you started, I've put together a list of eight tips a novice collector should keep in mind.

Let's jump right in, and start with the most important piece of advice…

1. Stay on top of the market you're invested in. All collectibles depend on three main factors: interest, scarcity and condition. Those are the biggies that span every area of the market, and each category demands that a collector be aware of the area they're invested in. So do your homework! That means keeping up on the latest trends, from current interests to the speculative market.

For example, many comic books shoot up in value once they've made it to the big screen. So there's an entire speculative market built around any superhero movies slotted for an upcoming release. I suggest joining a blog or online community that will keep you updated on your area. For instance, in our sports memorabilia report, we suggest joining Sports Collectors Daily, a blog devoted to delivering sports collecting news stories. You can also set up Google alerts to let you know whenever a key word/phrase is mentioned in a news story. Basically, make sure that you have a way to hear about a new development as soon as it occurs.

And for those of you who might like to step away from your computer, it's never a bad idea to familiarize yourself with a local collectibles store. The owners are on the ground floor, dealing with comics on a daily basis. It's the ideal environment for getting a better handle on which characters or issues are rising in demand. The same goes for trading card stores, etc.

You should also visit a local auction if you get the chance. It will give you a behind-the-scenes look at the auction process — and that will help you out immeasurably once you decide to sell your collectible. Plus, there are social network sites which not only connect you with fellow collectors, but also can be a source for finding items for sale.

That just covers interest — the first factor. As for **scarcity**, a little research will get you a long way. After you narrow down the items you're interested in, you should dig around to find out how many baseball cards come in a certain set, how many variant covers of a particular comic book issue were released, how many coins are in circulation, and so on. Basically, learn everything you can about the history and current status of your item. It'll give an idea of why people would want a certain collectible … and then you must ask yourself if this reason will always exist. That knowledge is a major factor when considering a buy.

Of course, there are also plenty of dealers and experts out there who are intimately acquainted with this knowledge, but it's never a bad idea to do your own research. As for finding your ideal dealer, I'll get to that in a moment. For now, just keep in mind that you will want to consult an expert, either when you're looking for an item or when you've already scored one and need to know the value.

Finally, you have to consider the **condition**. One tear, smudge or crease can mean thousands of dollars gone. On the other hand, a rare misprint could mean thousands more. So again, research is your friend! By learning everything you can about a collectible, you'll be able to get an idea of the value of various conditions.

For example, by looking up PSA Sports' trading card price guides, you can find the value PSA Sports assigns to a mint card, as opposed to a poor card. It's not much different to when researching the value of a car. Better condition vehicles can be worth more than poorly maintained vehicles. There are also price guides for just about any collectible you can imagine: comic books, coins, guitars, wines, movie posters, etc.

Ultimately, just remember this: Don't invest in collectibles when you aren't familiar with the market. If you're not interested enough in the hobby to spend some time each week — or at the very least each month — to keep up with the fluctuations in the market, you probably shouldn't invest in that hobby. It's no different than investing in stocks: In order to make the best of a trade, you have to keep up with the company.

2. Don't let emotions get in the way. Since this is an investing practice tied to hobbies and special areas of interest, emotions have a habit of getting in the way. For example, if your dad took you to every Mets game growing up, you'll probably have great memories of going to the ball park. Like getting a hot dog, while watching a player such as, say, future Hall of Fame pitcher Nolan Ryan walk across the field. Then you might be willing to spend an exorbitant amount just to own his glove — and end up paying much more than the value.

So you should always ask yourself this: What is the value of my collectible and will it appreciate?

The bottom line is that by admiring a collectible too much, you risk losing money. And if your goal is to make money, then too much admiration will get in the way of good decisions. If you really are investing, not collecting, don't let your emotions get in the way of your business sense.

While I recommend loving the item you get, you should also be logical. Refer to your research and/or a professional, and always remember that an item is an investment. Buy when it's cheap and sell when it's expensive. That's the long and short of it.

3. Find the best dealer. There are plenty of disreputable dealers out there, and fraud has been a problem in more than one area of the collectibles market. Know who you're buying from. Don't buy from eBay or an unknown auction house when you're first getting started. In fact, buy directly from the best dealer if possible — one you know you can trust. That means researching your candidate thoroughly.

Just a decade and a half to two decades ago, forged signatures and sales of fraudulent memorabilia of famous athletes were a rampant issue. In 2000, the FBI's Operation Bullpen revealed that $500 million to $900 million of autographed sports memorabilia were attributed to forgeries. In 2016, a man was charged in connection to a $2.5 million wire fraud scheme that involved an alleged five-year scheme of selling counterfeit and fraudulent sports memorabilia. This is why it is important to do your research and confirm authenticity.

So, many athletes now enter contract agreements with memorabilia retailers, where they promise to autograph items that will be sold only through that company. By doing your research, you can easily tell if a dealer has the right to sell a signed piece.

Of course, that's only for certain pieces of sports memorabilia. If you're in the market for another collectible area, though, doing your due diligence and researching the dealer will place you with a reputable company more often than not.

In the end, the old saying rings true here: If you come across a deal that seems too good to be true, it probably is.

4. Have your most valuable items professionally graded. As much research as you accomplish, you still want to have the experts take a look at your item. Professional grading means having an independent company assess the authenticity and condition of your item.

Grading can only increase the value, so the cost is normally worth it — specifically for any item with a value of $500 or more. For items of lesser value, the cost can become a significant part of an item's value, so it should be considered on a case-by-case basis.

And if you choose to do so, you can always discard the professional grading. It's not written in stone.

A professional service will also often seal it so that the condition can't be altered. For example, the Certified Guaranty Company (CGC) provides encapsulation storage that gives the optimum long-term protection for a comic book copy.

So this is something I stress: Professional grading is only helpful with your most valuable items.

5. Keep your collectible secure. As I mentioned, condition is key. The value of many collectibles is directly tied to the state of the item, and the reason makes sense. Since much of a collectible's value is tied to nostalgia — and is therefore based on emotional value — buyers are picky about the condition. That means if you improperly store an item, you can run the risk of losing your investment.

Again, I suggest getting a professional service to seal your item. And when considering storage, keep in mind the environment. A damp, humid environment is a comic book killer. Direct sunlight can fade your rare manuscripts or baseball cards, and so on. Remember that most categories of collectibles have price guides classifying how much an item is worth in pristine condition and what sort of damage degrades it, by what percentage of value. For instance, a well-read copy of "The Amazing Spider-Man No. 1" may be worth only 30% to 60% of the $6,000 list price, depending what degree of wear it displays.

You can prevent that type of scenario by learning how to properly store and treat your collectibles.

6. Plan your exit strategy. It's easy to fall in love with a purchase, hide it away and forget that you need to have an exit plan. Years can pass as your rare movie poster signed by Marilyn

Monroe gathers dust. Trends can come and go, and you may have missed your sterling opportunity to get the best price.

This ties directly back to my advice about staying on top of your market and about finding a reputable dealer. First off, being in the know means being knowledgeable enough to recognize the best opportunities for banking on your investment. So you always want to be up to date.

Second, you should have an idea of the dealer you want to use when you decide to sell. Dealers exist primarily to serve the needs of collectors — so investors should proceed with caution. Many investors do their research on which collectible to buy, and haggle with dealers to get the best possible price, but they forget to consider their exit options. When it's time to sell, they find that a large chunk of their profits are wiped out by an auctioneer's commission (which can go up to 25% oftentimes) or by dealer margins (often more than 50%).

So even when you first buy your collectible, plan an exit strategy. That way you're not hit with unexpected fees upon selling your collectible.

7. Diversify your investments. One of the reasons many investors get into collectibles is to diversify their portfolio. It's the basic rule of thumb: Never have all of your eggs in one basket. So, just as it doesn't make sense to have all of your money in stocks, it doesn't make sense to have all of your money in collectibles.

Figure out how much of your wealth you're willing to devote to collectibles, and stick to it.

8. Be patient. It's always nice when you can make an event-based stock trade and collect gains within a couple of weeks or months. Well, the collectibles market oftentimes doesn't work that way. Collectibles are simply not an avenue for immediate profits. They can take years to surge in value, even decades. Of course, there are those happy moments when you buy the first issue of an obscure comic series right before the movie gets announced and the comic's value soars. But that's not something to bank on because it's a fairly rare event.

When collecting, you generally have to think in terms of a five to 15 year plan in order to realize profits. Just be patient, and remember that you should love what you're buying in the event that you're stuck with your item. I always like to think that if I'm buying what appeals to me, there's probably someone else to whom it will appeal as well. It's a win-win.

A Final Note

If there's one message when starting your collection, it's this: Do your homework, buy what you love, deal with reputable people and have fun with it. That's the collectibles market boiled down.

Although this can be an area that requires some time and effort, it's clearly a great hobby that can reward you with fantastic profits. And it's an ideal way to diversify your portfolio with inflation-proof wealth while doing something you genuinely enjoy. I can't think of many investment areas with that definition.

INCOME SECRET NO. 10:

The Low-Cost Maneuver to
Defeat Disaster ... *Trust* Me

Do you like horror stories? Good ... because the world of asset protection is full of them.

Here's a doozy. It involves a couple I met via an ex-colleague, just as I was transitioning from the nonprofit world to writing about sovereignty and asset protection.

Belinda and Ryan were at that stage in life where everything is starting to come together ... just bought a home, student loans paid off, careers looking good, bun in the oven. Nice folks.

When I met them, though, they were pale with stress and worry.

Besides their new Atlanta home, Belinda and Ryan also owned a couple of inherited properties, one on the East Coast and one in the Rockies. They were also passive co-owners of a thriving business, managed by Belinda's brother. Belinda's dad, who had started the business, had left Belinda a fair chunk of money, which was doing nothing in particular in a bank account except serving as collateral for a loan they'd taken to renovate their new house.

Those renovations included construction of a new retaining wall at the back of their house, which overlooked a wooded stream, so common in Atlanta. A few days after a torrential downpour had swollen that stream a bit more than usual, the partially completed retaining wall collapsed on a workman, killing him instantly.

Unbeknownst to them, the contractor they'd hired — at the recommendation of their architect — had no business liability insurance. Belinda and Ryan were therefore *personally* responsible for restitution to the man's family.

When I met them, they faced a multimillion-dollar lawsuit that would force them to sell almost everything they owned ... including their new house and their share of the business, which meant liquidating it entirely, drawing Belinda's brother into the turmoil and straining the family.

Two sadder faces I will likely never see. Almost there ... now, nothing.

But the really sad thing is that it didn't have to be like that.

A simple, quick, low-cost legal maneuver would have put the bulk of their assets out of reach of that lawsuit. Their real estate, their business and their bank balances would have been safe. They'd have had to pay something, but their legal shield would have led to a quick and more reasonable settlement amount.

Nobody knows where lightning may strike. But strike it does, thousands of times a day, all over the country. Sometimes it does real damage. The odds of a lawsuit like the one against Belinda and Ryan, however, are far greater than those of a light-ning strike. The U.S. has 80% of the world's lawyers. They file over 15 million tort suits in U.S. courts every year. Fifty-five percent of those are found in favor of the plaintiff. You have a 1 in 5 chance of being sued in any given year, unless you're in medical practice, a business owner or a landlord, in which case it's much higher.

But what if "you" and "your assets" can't be sued at the same time? A potential plaintiff can only claim what you own person-ally. If most of "your" assets aren't actually "yours," you're not much of a target.

For a few thousand dollars, you can make that happen ... and protect yourself from Belinda and Ryan's fate.

In Trusts We Trust ... Up to a Point

The Anglo-American legal tradition is rich in mechanisms that protect personal assets so that people can focus on wealth building instead of wealth defense. There are lots of ways to reduce the risk of personal loss, thereby increasing the attrac-tiveness of innovative business activity.

One of these mechanisms is the trust. The concept of a "trust" is fundamentally very simple: One person holds legal title to an asset for another. If I transfer the title of the family business to you, and say, "Hold this business for the benefit of my family," then a trust has been created.

The basic trust has four components:

1. The person who creates the trust (the "settlor" or "grantor").

2. The trust itself and its assets.

3. The person who controls the trust and its assets ("trustee").

4. Those who are to receive the benefits of those assets ("beneficiaries").

The concept of the trust has expanded greatly over the centuries. Large financial institutions often hold billions of dollars in trust for families all over the world. There are now many types of trusts: revocable and irrevocable trusts, grantor trusts, qualified trusts, lead trusts, life insurance and annuity trusts, unit trusts, and even the bizarre "intentionally defective trust."

An asset protection trust (APT) is a trust that protects the trust assets from potential future creditors and liabilities of the beneficiaries. That is, as long as the assets are in a properly formed trust, they are not the personal property of the beneficiaries, and therefore not subject to claims arising from the beneficiaries' debts, including those generated from lawsuits, like the one against Belinda and Ryan.

Unlike a traditional revocable living trust, an APT must be an irrevocable trust. This is critical, because a creditor can come after any assets over which you have control.

A revocable living trust, by design, is one in which you have control over the assets. You can terminate the trust, withdraw funds and so on. A creditor who is awarded a claim against you would have the same ability to withdraw trust assets or funds to pay the claim. Your assets are not protected at all.

But in a traditional irrevocable trust, you relinquish any right to the assets and have no control over them. If you don't have control and can't benefit from or withdraw the assets, your creditors can't either. Your assets are safe.

Traditionally, this is achieved in a trust through inclusion of a "spendthrift provision" in an irrevocable trust that prohibits creditors from making claims against a beneficiary's interest in the trust, and prevents the beneficiaries from transferring or pledging their interests in the trust to someone else, such as a creditor. Even if you wanted to settle with a creditor, the provisions of the irrevocable trust wouldn't permit it.

This "spendthrift provision" protection, however, is generally unavailable to the creator of the trust — the "settlor" who donates its initial assets. If you establish a trust of which you are also a beneficiary — a so-called "self-settled trust" — the trust is generally ignored for purposes of the creator/beneficiary's debts and liabilities, and your assets are unprotected.

In other words, the only way trust assets could be protected from your potential creditors as creator of the trust is for you, as the settlor, to give up complete control of and benefit from the trust and its assets. That means, for example, that you couldn't put the family home into such a trust and live in it, or profit from a business held in trust.

So it seems you face a choice of a trust where you can't access the assets at all or one where you can, but they aren't protected from creditors. Clearly, what's needed is a way to put assets into an irrevocable trust, so creditors can't access them, but still be a beneficiary of the trust's assets — say, your house, investment accounts or shares in a family business.

This is where the domestic asset protection trust (DAPT) comes in. A DAPT allows the trust creator, the settlor, to be a discretionary beneficiary, and yet the trust assets are still protected from the settlor's creditors. That's why, in the past, in order to obtain such protections, U.S. citizens often looked to offshore jurisdictions that permit spendthrift trusts that also allow the settlor to be a beneficiary, and thereby be protected from creditors.

Do the Nevada 2-Step

In 1999, the Nevada Legislature amended its trust statute to permit self-settled, first-party spendthrift trusts, commonly referred to as a Nevada asset protection trust (NAPT). Under this law, as long as the settlors strictly comply with statutory requirements, they can name themselves as beneficiaries of their own trusts and enjoy the same creditor protection as third-party beneficiaries of the trust. Problem solved.

It is important to remember that an NAPT is an irrevocable trust. Once a traditional irrevocable trust is established, the settlor cannot take back the assets and terminate the trust, or even change how they are distributed — you can't change your mind later.

But Nevada law allows you, as the settlor, to keep the ability to change where the trust assets are ultimately distributed — "the power of appointment." That means you can change who the final beneficiaries are, or how the assets are distributed.

There's more. With a traditional trust, a single trustee is responsible for making distributions from the trust, taking care of all administrative matters (such as filing tax returns and bookkeeping) and overseeing investment and management of the trust assets.

That means giving up control to someone else, even if you are one of the beneficiaries of the trust. You couldn't run your own business or manage your investment portfolio, for example.

But another unique feature of the NAPT is that the powers and duties of the trustee can be allocated to more than one trustee. As a result, you, as the settlor, can also serve as a trustee of the trust.

This is important because Nevada law restricts the settlor from being the sole trustee or having the power to make distributions to himself. The settlor can only serve as a trustee of the trust with the authority to invest and manage the trust assets. Someone else — a second trustee — has to make any distributions that benefit the settlor, such as allowing him or her to live in a property or receive profits from a business held in trust.

With this in mind, Nevada law requires that if a non-Nevada resident is establishing an NAPT, one of the trustees must be a resident of Nevada — the trustee who takes care of the general administrative tasks and makes any distributions to the settlor/ trustee/beneficiary.

The only limitation is that this second, Nevada-based trustee cannot be required by the terms of the trust to make distributions to the settlor. While this seems like a limitation, it is outweighed by the benefits of the powers and controls you as the settlor can retain while still having creditor protection.

Timing Is Everything

When it comes to investment, we all know that timing is critical. The same is true for asset protection trusts.

When you first hear about them, APTs sound almost magical. With the wave of a hand (OK, the stroke of a pen), your assets are legally no longer yours — but you can keep using them as if they were!

This is sort of magical, but there's an important caveat: The trick doesn't work if you are aware of an impending claim against you.

Let's say Belinda and Ryan called a lawyer and set up an APT the day after the accident that killed the workman happened. They knew what was coming so they moved to protect their wealth.

Nothing would stop them from setting up such an APT, but for the purposes of any lawsuit arising from the workman's death, it would be useless. That's because the transfer of assets to their new APT would be regarded as a "fraudulent conveyance."

A fraudulent conveyance is a transfer of an asset with the intent to hinder, delay or defraud a creditor. Just like you can't buy insurance after an accident has happened, you can't transfer assets to an APT and have them protected by it once you know they will be pursued by a creditor — even if the lawsuit hasn't even been filed yet.

This is where the NAPT is unquestionably the best of its kind in the U.S.

Specifically, under Nevada law, if a creditor was a creditor of the settlor at the time the settlor made the transfer to an NAPT, the creditor must commence an action to challenge the transfer within the later of (a) two years after the transfer, or (b) six months after the creditor discovers — or reasonably should have discovered — the transfer.

A creditor who was not a creditor of the settlor at the time the settlor made the transfer to an NAPT must commence an action to challenge the transfer within two years of the transfer. If a creditor does not bring a claim against the settlor within the prescribed period, the claim is barred.

This two-year statute of limitations on fraudulent conveyance for NAPTs is one of the shortest in the country. Note that the act that starts the statute of limitations running is the transfer of assets from the settlor to the NAPT. Therefore, each time assets are transferred to the NAPT, a new transfer has occurred, and the statute will begin to run on a claim against that specific asset.

Even if the statute of limitations does not bar the claim, the creditor is required to show that the transfer was a fraudulent conveyance. This may be difficult for the creditor to prove, especially if the creditor's claim arose after the transfer of assets to an NAPT.

7 Additional Benefits

In 2009, the Nevada legislature passed important changes affecting NAPTs. These include some critical enhancements:

- The trustee of an NAPT can "decant" or transfer the trust property to a second trust with different provisions, without first obtaining court approval.

- "Directed trusts" are allowed, which permit the delegation of the trustee's investment powers over the trust's assets to a third-party investment adviser.

- "Trust protectors" are allowed. These are nontrustees who have certain discretionary powers over an otherwise irrevocable trust.

- No "exception creditors" are allowed. Previously, divorcing spouses' claims against an NAPT were not included in the trust protections. Now they are.

Here's what that means for you — in addition to some pre-existing benefits of the NAPT:

Decanting

"Decanting" a trust is when the trustee distributes the trust's assets into a different trust with different terms for one or more of the same beneficiaries of the original trust. In most cases, this second trust is brand-new. Traditionally, this requires the permission of a judge, since it could easily be used to defeat the purpose of the original trust.

Nevada has traditionally been one of the most innovative states when it comes to decanting. In 2015, Nevada legislators approved SB484, which essentially gives an NAPT trustee a "do-over" to make changes to trust terms that traditionally would not have been permitted without a judge's permission.

Most importantly, it is now possible to decant an NAPT to remove a mandatory income distribution under the terms of the original NAPT. This creates two opportunities.

First, it allows a trustee — which, remember, can be the settlor, i.e., you — to decant trust assets that were subject to a mandatory income distribution under the original NAPT to a new trust where they are not. For example, if the original NAPT called for trust-investment income to be directed to a child or spouse who has become alienated from the settlor, the investments that generate this income can be decanted to a new trust that does not contain such a provision.

Second, if an NAPT is designed to direct all income to one particular beneficiary, there is no ability to shift income to the lower federal and state income tax brackets of other trust beneficiaries, or to retain income in the trust for taxes that the beneficiary must pay if receiving the distribution. Decanting income-producing assets to a second trust overcomes this by changing the terms of distributions.

Investment Advisers

As I often recommend in the case of offshore trusts and limited liability companies (LLCs), an investment adviser can play an important role in maximizing the investment returns of your assets.

If you're lucky, the Nevada-based trustee for your NAPT can do this. But in most cases — especially where the settlor, as second trustee, has investment expertise — it's too much to expect the trustee to handle this. In such cases, Nevada law allows you to appoint an investment adviser who is authorized under the terms of the trust to advise the trustees on investment decisions. This could easily be someone with whom you already work and in whom you have established trust.

The Trust Protector

The requirement that one trustee of an NAPT be a Nevada-based person is central to the legislature's intentions, which was to make the state a center of business incorporation and associated services. But, as with any relationship with a potential stranger, you can never be entirely certain that you'll always see eye-to-eye … or that the trustee won't abuse his position to enrich himself through excessive fees, etc.

To deal with this, Nevada trust law allows an innovation that originally appeared in offshore APTs — the "trust protector" or often just "protector." The idea behind the protector is to have somebody who can watch over the trustee, and terminate the trustee for any misconduct.

Nevada law incorporates all the experience of offshore APTs in this regard. Originally, the only power the protector had was to fire the trustee. But as offshore APTs evolved, protectors were sometimes given additional powers, such as to appoint the successor trustee if one was fired. This creates the theoretical threat if the protector has the power to both fire and appoint a trustee, the protector might appoint herself as the trustee. Thus, offshore APTs further evolved to prohibit a protector from being the trustee or appointing somebody close to the protector.

All trusts should have a protector — even if you are the trustee and beneficiary of your own trust. This seems odd: You get to control and use the trust assets freely while you are alive, so why would you need a protector?

The problem is that you will eventually die, and whoever you have appointed as the successor trustee in your trust document will become the acting trustee. It's this trustee you have to worry about — with you gone, this new trustee could potentially abuse the trust for fees, leaving the beneficiaries with no recourse except to engage in expensive litigation. With a protector, the misbehaving trustee can be fired.

No Exceptions!

All other U.S. states provide for some type of "exception creditors," typically as divorcing spouses or pre-existing tort claims. Essentially, this means that in such jurisdictions, even if you have made it past the statute of limitations and there are no fraudulent conveyance issues, the exception creditor could still get at the trust's assets.

Nevada is the only U.S. jurisdiction that does not allow exception creditors. This has made NAPTs an alternative to prenuptial agreements — by agreeing to put assets in an NAPT, prospective spouses are essentially agreeing to surrender their right to attach them absent common agreement. By acting before marriage, you're basically stashing away a "nest egg," and setting aside a certain amount of your assets to be protected in the event the relationship unexpectedly terminates — notwithstanding your hope and expectations to the contrary.

This is nice, but NAPT planning related to marriage shouldn't wait until right before a divorce — or even during a marriage. That's because establishing an NAPT might be regarded as a fraudulent transfer, a breach of a fiduciary duty owed by one spouse to the other.

Taxation

Because the settlor retains powers and controls in an NAPT, the trust is treated as a "grantor trust" for tax purposes. This means that all income and losses of the trust pass through and are reported by the settlor on his or her tax return; there are no additional taxes; and you retain any personal tax deductions.

Similarly, because transfers into an NAPT are not regarded as a "completed" gift, there are no gift tax implications — unless you design it so that transfers to the trust are treated as completed gifts and therefore excluded from your estate.

The values of the NAPT assets, however, are included in the settlor's estate for estate tax purposes … unless you adopt the next nifty trick.

Dynasty Trusts

A dynasty trust is a trust designed to avoid or minimize estate taxes on wealth transfers to subsequent generations. By holding assets in the trust and making well-defined distributions to each generation, the entire wealth of the trust is not subject to estate taxes with the passage of each generation.

Dynasty trusts avoid the generation-skipping transfer tax that occurs when traditional trusts attempt to bypass transferring all assets to spouses or children — for example, reserving property assets to one's great-great-great-great grandchildren, to be held in trust for them, but not fully owned, by the intervening generations.

In most cases, the common law rule against "perpetuities" forbids any legal instrument — contracts, wills, trusts and so on — from tying up property for too long a time beyond the lives of people living when the instrument was written. (Charitable remainder trusts are excepted.) For example, the head of a family might stipulate in a trust document that assets be used in a certain way forever, preventing a spouse or heirs from accessing them after his death.

The common-law tradition is that any heritable "interest" must vest to heirs no later than 21 years after the death of the last identifiable individual living at the time the interest was created. A 2005 Nevada law, however, explicitly allowed for dynasty trusts that can last for 365 years — thus permitting skipping many generations for estate tax purposes.

Although this was challenged, the Nevada Supreme Court ruled in March 2015, in the case of *Bullion Monarch Mining Inc. v. Barrick Goldstrike Mines Inc.*, that the 365-year perpetuities law is the law in Nevada.

Combining an NAPT With a Limited Liability Company

The limited liability company (LLC) format provides an excellent form of protection, especially for real estate holdings. There's nothing stopping you from creating an LLC to hold certain assets under an NAPT — and plenty of advantages to doing so.

Here's why. All states permit personal creditors of an LLC member (i.e., owner) to obtain a "charging order" from a court against the debtor-owner's "membership interest" — i.e., their proceeds from the LLC's operation, such as rental income from properties owned by it. But most states' charging orders only give creditors the debtor-member's "financial rights." A creditor with a charging order doesn't get to participate in LLC management, so they can't order a distribution of cash or liquidation of assets.

So if the LLC members direct the LLC manager not to make a distribution to the debtor-member, or refuse to sell the real estate in question, the creditor is stuck. Moreover, because a creditor with a charging order has the debtor-member's "financial rights," the IRS could hold the creditor responsible for taxes on the debtor-member's share of LLC profits — regardless of whether or not any profit distributions are made! That makes lawsuits against assets owned by a properly constituted LLC very unattractive indeed.

The problem is that many states allow alternative remedies for creditors beyond the charging order. Such remedies are known as "piercing the veil," since they allow the creditor or litigant to get directly at the LLC's members. Not Nevada. Charging-order protection is the exclusive remedy for the creditor of a member of a Nevada LLC. Nevada also allows single-member LLCs, which receive the same protection from charging orders and multimember LLCs. That means the trustee of your NAPT could also be the sole member of an LLC owned by the trust, in which you could hold rental properties, for example. This LLC will protect the other assets held by it from any claims or liabilities arising from other assets owned by it.

How an NAPT Could Have Helped Belinda and Ryan

If Belinda and Ryan had placed their home, other properties, business interests and inherited cash assets in an NAPT, they would have been insulated from the lawsuit brought by the workman's family.

The spendthrift provision inherent in the nature of the irrevocable NAPT would have prevented either of them from agreeing to attachment of assets in trust, even if they wanted to do so.

Of course, this would have entailed some careful planning. For example, Belinda and Ryan's own home and inherited bank accounts would need to be owned directly by the NAPT, which would insulate them from liquidation (as would Georgia's homestead exemption for personal residences).

Their other two inherited properties should be in an LLC owned by the trust, set up specifically as a "series" LLC, which insulates each property for liabilities arising from the other. Their shares in the family business managed by their brother could have been in a separate trust-owned LLC.

Having an NAPT doesn't mean Belinda and Ryan could dispense with liability insurance on their home, however.

After all, the legal fees to defend against the lawsuit would need to be paid, and without insurance, any award to the plaintiff would require liquidating assets not owned by the trust, like vehicles, furniture and other personal items.

A Special Deal on the NAPT

The NAPT is a great vehicle for domestic asset protection. It can do almost everything that an offshore APT can do, at a fraction of the cost.

This makes the NAPT ideal for folks who want a low-cost, quick, easily manageable route to strong domestic asset protection. And as an exclusive for my readers, I've managed to secure a great deal on getting one set up.

My good friend, attorney Josh Bennett, will set up a properly constituted NAPT for an all-inclusive cost of $12,500. That's about half of what you'd normally pay. That includes all of the first-year setup and registration costs, including drafting the trust document, appointing a Nevada-based trustee and completing all the requisite paperwork.

Now, you will find offers for rough-and-ready NAPTs on the Internet. Don't do it.

As should be clear from what I've shared with you here, it is critical to have an experienced, qualified attorney draft the specific trust agreement and other documents that you need to address your particular needs. You're not going to get that off the internet.

Instead, I strongly encourage you to contact Josh to get started on your personal asset protection plan right away … after all, you can never know if and when the lightning bolt that struck Belinda and Ryan will strike you.

Contact:

Josh N. Bennett, Esq.
440 North Andrews Avenue
Fort Lauderdale, FL 33301
Tel.: (954) 779-1661
Mobile: (786) 202-5674
Email: josh@joshbennett.com
Website: www.joshbennett.com

TAXES

No one likes paying taxes. Every year, it feels like the tax-man takes a bigger and bigger chunk out of your earnings. But there are some key steps you can take right now to lower your tax obligation so that you keep more of your hard-earned dollars in your wallet. In fact, this section contains a tip that would help you to legally stop paying U.S. taxes completely. Improving the income in your life means taking control of your taxes.

INCOME SECRET NO. 11:

Stop Giving Interest-Free Loans to Uncle Sam

People love the idea of a tax refund. It's free money, a windfall.

Nearly 80% of taxpayers get a refund after they file. Then they spend it on new mattresses, car down payments or a vacation.

If you got a tiny refund, that's understandable; taxes are hard to predict in advance.

If you get a big one every year, however, then you are missing a chance to cut your taxes by lowering your tax withholding (this is the W-4 form at work) and instead putting that money into a 401(k) or individual retirement account (IRA).

It's a cliché, but it's true. By taking the refund, you essentially have loaned the government money all year interest-free.

The IRS doesn't hide this fact. In 2017, it reportedly refunded $324 billion to taxpayers, averaging $2,895.

Invested in a Treasury bill at 2%, that's $6.5 billion in free money we give to Uncle Sam for no reason except our fear of owing taxes.

Put another way, that's a whole year of car payments given up by the average taxpayer because thinking for five minutes about your likely tax bill for the year is too hard.

If you're getting a sizeable refund every year, contact the accounting or human resources department of your employer to adjust the withholding on your W-4 form — now.

Put that money to work *for you* rather than as an interest-free loan to the government.

INCOME SECRET NO. 12:

Double Your Tax Break With a Spousal IRA

Proper planning for retirement not only gives you a nice nest egg on which to survive and enjoy your golden years, but it actually helps you lower tax burdens and save some money right now.

If you're already contributing to a 401(k), your next step is to open a traditional IRA immediately. You can always put money into an IRA, even if you have a workplace plan. The question is whether it's deductible, and that's a matter of your income level and how much you already put into your workplace plan.

For couples, the deduction for an IRA contribution begins to fade after a modified adjusted gross income of $101,000 — if you are covered by retirement plans at work — and then you get a partial deduction if you earn more. If you are not and your spouse is not, the income limit is $189,000. Pretty high. (Note: these amounts can change each year, so check the www.irs.gov website for updates.)

If you have previous 401(k) plans, you can roll them over into the IRA to grow the balance and manage them more coherently.

With a traditional IRA, you can contribute up to $5,500 a year if you're under 50. The limit bumps up to $6,500 if you're older than 50. That's a nice deduction you can claim at the end of the year if you're making under $101,000.

But what if you're the sole breadwinner and your spouse is unemployed or underemployed?

You can put money into his or her IRA up to the annual limit of $5,500 (add another $1,000 if your spouse is over 50).

Effectively, you get to double the IRA contribution as a couple even though only one of you earns a salary. This money comes off your joint taxable income and pushes you even further down in the tax brackets.

INCOME SECRET NO. 13:

Pocket Extra Income Taking Advantage of President Trump's Favorite Tax Loophole (TAX)

For most of my working life, I've been a contractor.

No, I don't build or remodel houses.

I just wasn't directly employed by the people who paid me. Instead, I sold my services to them as a product.

Sometimes my relationship with my clients was at arm's length. I did contractual work at a per-piece rate. Other times, I received a regular retainer under long-term contracts.

No matter the format, this setup had several things in common:

1. I managed my financial affairs — and my taxes — as a business separate from my household.

I had business income and expenses that were separate from my personal finances. My personal income was whatever was left over.

2. I was responsible for calculating and paying my own taxes on that "leftover" income. My clients didn't withhold anything or hand it over to the government. I did that myself, every quarter.

3. Nobody told me how, where or when to do my work. I always cooperated with my clients' reasonable requests, of course … but the final call was always mine.

The lifestyle had its pros and cons.

The main downside was that my income fluctuated.

I had to maintain a healthy reserve of cash to meet my personal expenses. I also had to manage my commercial reputation, which is quite different from workplace relationships.

But the pros outweighed the cons. I was — and, above all, felt — independent. I had more control over my income and work effort. My time was flexible.

I worked from home most of the time ... and no commute!

But the main advantage was the leverage being an independent contractor gave me over the taxman.

This "Income Secret" — prompted by the recent tax bill passed by Congress and signed by the president — will show you:

- How the new tax code creates huge advantages for self-employed, incorporated individuals.

- When it makes sense to set yourself up as a "business" ... even if you're currently an employee.

- Why you should get expert advice and where to seek that advice.

You see, the revised tax code — which was supposed to be fairer and simpler — in fact, creates several hacks that allow some people to pay less taxes than others doing the same work.

These hacks are hugely contentious in the tax community ... but they are now legal and far from simple.

My goal here is to give you an accessible summary of these new tax opportunities so you can decide whether they make sense for you.

As is the basis for my subscription service, *The Bauman Letter*, I want to show you how to take advantage of any opportunity to enhance your income and protect your wealth!

Pass-Through to Heaven

During halftime of the recent Georgia-Alabama national college championship game here in Atlanta (sorry, Dawgs!), I asked my pal Joey if he knew what a "pass-through" was.

He thought it had something to do with digestion. Nice try, Joey, but no cigar.

In U.S. tax parlance, a pass-through is any corporate entity that pays no corporate income tax. All a pass-through entity's profits "pass-through" to the owner(s), who pay income tax on those profits as an individual. (Lawyers call them "disregarded entities" because they are ignored for tax purposes.)

This contrasts with C-Corporations, which pay tax directly on their own account, which is separate from their shareholders, who pay tax on dividends.

Pass-through entities (PTEs) include sole proprietorships, partnerships, limited liability companies (LLCs) and subchapter S-Corporations.

Up until now, the owners of such businesses have paid tax on their net income at individual rates.

But the tax law that went into effect on January 1, 2018 effectively lowers the tax rate on PTE income to well below the individual rate. This creates a big opportunity for you.

Not Quite the Same as the Old Boss

Those who drafted the new tax law had to change the way PTEs are handled.

The new top U.S. corporate tax rate — levied on shareholder-owned C-Corporations — is 21%. If Congress had left the treatment of PTEs as it was, their owners would pay much more tax than C-Corporations because the top five individual tax brackets are well above 21% — 22%, 24%, 32%, 35% and 37%.

Now, let's be clear: many PTEs aren't small businesses owned by Main Street Americans who would be cruelly disadvantaged by paying more tax on their profits than corporate behemoths.

In fact, 70% of PTE equity is in multimillion-dollar businesses. PTE structures are especially common in finance and real estate. Almost all of President Trump's businesses, for example, are organized as LLCs. More than two-thirds of all U.S. PTE income goes to the top 1% of U.S. households by income.

Nevertheless, the average small businessperson would be enraged if they had to continue to pay taxes on their profits at individual rates while the corporate rate was slashed to 21%.

Congress' solution to this political problem creates an opportunity for significant tax savings for those of us who aren't multimillionaires.

As I mentioned, until January 1, 2018, PTE income was taxed as personal income, up to 39.6%.

But the new rules grant a 20% deduction for "qualified business income" (QBI) ... PTE owners can now simply deduct 20% of their businesses' income from their taxable income, and pay no tax on it.

For many people, this results in a big tax cut compared to the previous pass-through system.

For example, let's say you are married filing jointly and employed as a senior electrician at an annual salary is $75,000. Under the new tax brackets, your tax will be $7,233, or 9.64%.

If you create a PTE, however, and pay yourself an annual salary of $12,000, your tax under the new system will be $5,721, or 7.63%.

This also creates a paradoxical situation for owners of PTEs. Under the new rules, if you're a PTE owner and you want to pay less tax, pay yourself the smallest possible salary (since it's taxed at individual rates) and push as much income as possible in the qualified business income category (so you can deduct 20% of it from your taxable income).

Instantly, "qualified business income" becomes hugely important. Just what is QBI?

QBI is "the net amount of items of income, gain, deduction and loss with respect to your trade or business." In other words, it's your business' profit ... what's left after you've paid all your operating costs, including your own salary.

(Of course, if QBI is less than zero, it's treated as a loss from a qualified business in the following year, and can be used to offset your taxes then.)

Under the new rules, in other words, the more business income you can shoehorn into QBI, the more you can save on tax, since 20% of that amount is now tax free.

It gets even better.

You've probably heard that there is now a $10,000 cap on the deductibility of state and local income and property taxes. That's going to hurt folks who pay a lot of those taxes.

But PTEs can deduct the full amount of any state and local taxes they pay as a business expense. That home office makes a lot more sense now ... you'll be able to use it to reduce your nondeductible personal property taxes by shifting some of it to your business accounts.

Naturally, there are some catches.

First, QBI excludes passive income such as capital gains, dividends and interest income (unless the interest is received in connection with a lending business). You can't put your brokerage accounts into a PTE and get 20% of your returns tax free.

Second, the new 20% QBI deduction phases out for individuals who make more than $157,500 a year, or $315,000 for joint filers — with an important exception, as I'll show you below.

Third, the QBI deduction is limited to PTEs that provide a "specified service trade or business."

If your PTE provides services in health, law, consulting, athletics, financial services, brokerage services or anything "principally relying on the reputation or skill of one or more of its employees or owners" (except, for some unfathomable reason, architects and engineers), you're not invited to the party.

The new tax law calls such excluded occupations "listed professions." Even if you are in one of them, however, if your taxable income is under $157,500 individual/$315,000 joint, then you can take the full 20% QBI deduction. After that, the deduction phases out through a complicated formula until you hit $207,500 individual/$415,000 joint, at which point you lose the deduction completely and the old rules apply ... you pay tax at the individual rate.

Finally, even if you exceed this income cap, you can take another form of QBI deduction depending on how many employees and/or how much capital your PTE has.

Simpler? Hah!

So much for filing your tax return on a postcard.

In this next section, I'm going to expand a bit on two typical types of PTEs. For simplicity, I'm going to call them the "Independent Professional" and the "Corker Rule" cases.

The Independent Professional

This version of the PTE tax break is aimed at people who have few employees — perhaps only themselves as a single employee — or a small partnership. It's limited by income to prevent high-earners from declaring themselves "consultants" to escape tax. The rationale is that if you are contributing mainly your labor and not much capital, and/or not creating many jobs, then you can access the deduction only if your income is below certain thresholds.

Here's how it works.

For people in non-listed professions and for those in listed professions earning under the thresholds above: If your taxable income is below $157,500 individual/$315,000 joint, the tax-free portion of QBI for any PTE you own is simply 20%.

So, if your income is $100,000 and your QBI is $75,000, then your deduction is $15,000, or 20% of your QBI. You don't pay any tax on that income. Period.

As I explained above, you can continue to take a partial, pro-rated QBI deduction until you hit $207,500 individual/$415,000 joint taxable income.

The Corker Rule

All is not lost if you are above the threshold amounts, however. Two further types of PTEs can join the game:

- You have a multimillion-dollar LLC that has a dozen or so employees — say, a car dealership. You pull in a decent six-figure income, so you're above the $207,500 individual/$415,000 joint taxable income cap.

- You have an LLC with a lot of equity in real estate but few employees. Again, your taxable income is above the cap.

In both cases, you have the option of calculating your QBI deduction as the greater of:

1. 50% of W-2 wages paid by your PTE, including your own, or...

2. The sum of 25% of W-2 wages paid by your PTE plus 2.5% of the original, undepreciated value of all qualified property. Qualified property is physical property used to produce QBI available for use in your PTE at the end of the tax year. This includes all capital equipment ... and, significantly, real estate.

For example, let's assume your car dealership pays $250,000 in W-2 wages, and owns a building worth $1 million.

- Under the first option, 50% of W-2 wages equals $125,000.

- Under the second option, 25% of W-2 wages plus 2.5% of unadjusted basis of your qualified property is $62,000 plus $25,000 equals $90,000.

So, your best option is to use the first method and declare $125,000 of your QBI as nontaxable income.

In the second case, let's say you're a real estate mogul like President Trump (or Senator Bob Corker of Tennessee, after whom this rule is named. He changed his vote from a "nay" to a "yea" after this option was slipped into the bill at the last minute). You have few employees and a small W-2 wage bill of $50,000, but your PTE owns $50 million worth of hotels, office buildings, condos and so on.

- Under the first option, 50% of W-2 wages equals $25,000.

- Under the second option, 25% of W-2 wages plus 2.5% of unadjusted basis of your qualified property is $12,500 plus $1,250,000 equals $1,262,500.

I'm sure I don't need to tell you which deduction you're going to take in that case.

The Corker Rule — which was clearly created to benefit multimillionaires, including the authors of the bill — creates an intriguing angle for us lesser mortals, and it's a biggie.

2018: Year of the Tax Lawyer

All the profit-shifting shenanigans that multinationals engage in will now be relevant for domestic businesses.

That quote comes from a document called "The Games They Will Play," an evolving analysis of the new tax law by a group of top tax-law professors.

The professors are right. The new tax treatment of PTEs is a windfall for lawyers who design and create LLCs, partnerships and S-Corporations.

Remember that the new tax treatment of PTEs doesn't apply to "specified service trades or businesses." These "listed professionals" include doctors, lawyers, financial consultants, etc.

If they earn too much, these poor souls aren't allowed to take advantage of the 20% QBI deduction! Rats!

But the Corker Rule creates a new quiver of lawyerly tricks ... and I predict it's going to generate a lot of traffic at state company registration offices around the country this year.

Here's why:

Assume you're a partner in a law firm called LawFirm LLC. You and your partners form SideCar LLC, contributing some capital and using it to buy and hold the building you currently rent. SideCar LLC rents the building back to LawFirm LLC at an above- market rent.

BOOM! You suddenly have qualified "Corker Rule" income in a real estate PTE! Before, you were shut out of the game because you practiced a listed profession. By splitting your business into parts, you save on tax.

All it took was some company formation work, and you're sending less to the IRS.

This is the same as the "transfer pricing" trick U.S. multinationals use to shift income from U.S. to foreign subsidiaries. Create a foreign subsidiary and transfer something of value that your business uses to it — say, Apple's patent on the iPhone — then have the subsidiary rent it back to you at an inflated cost.

That slashes your taxable income in a high- tax situation (Apple, Inc., subject to U.S. corporate tax) and shifts income to a low-tax situation (Apple Cayman Islands, Inc., paying little to no tax).

Now, under the new law "listed professionals" can play the same game. Just split an existing PTE into an unqualified (high-tax) professional PTE and one or more qualified (low-tax) PTEs.

The low-tax PTEs then can charge fees to the high-tax professional PTE — for example, rent for office space, secretarial services, a medical practice's X-ray operation ... even interest on loans from one PTE to another. Those business-to-business payments reduce QBI for the disqualified PTE and shift it to the PTE that can use the 50% W-2 wage or Corker Rule deductions ... just like Apple does when it parks its patents in a foreign subsidiary in a low tax jurisdiction.

Bam. Doctors and lawyers are now in the real estate business!

There are other ways to hack the new system. The tax professors who wrote "The Games They Will Play" say, "borrow(ing) from the terminology of gerrymandering strategies, let's call them 'cracking' and 'packing.'"

- Cracking. The first strategy is to "crack" apart the revenue streams from an existing PTE, so as much income as possible can qualify for the deduction. The anecdote above referred to the real estate angle.

  But "listed" professionals could also form separate service — providing PTEs providing non-listed services — PTEs handling their accounting, document management, software, secretarial services and so on. Again, the game would be to overcharge the main PTE for these services and manipulate the two alternative QBI deduction methods to minimize taxes.

- Packing. The second strategy is to "pack" qualifying professional activities into a PTE to transform it into one that isn't primarily providing a "listed" service.

  For example, real estate lawyers might both provide legal advice and manage real estate — mixing the businesses so that the IRS can't distinguish them to get the 20% PTE deduction for the whole operation.

  Another route is for a "listed" professional simply to join a PTE that doesn't provide "listed" services. For example, a lawyer that becomes a partner in a PTE that does real estate development could take advantage of the exception for "architecture" or "engineering" PTEs.

Finally, the new treatment of PTEs creates an opportunity for employees of PTEs, too. For example, associates at law firms could band together into what the professors call "Associates, LLC — a separate partnership paid to provide services to the original firm." Each associate might then qualify for the 20% QBI deduction.

Now you see why I say that 2018 is going to be the year of the tax attorney.

Does it Make Sense?

I can hear you thinking, "Wow, Ted, this is fascinating. But it seems like a lot of effort!"

True. But for some of you, the time to act is now — you only get the new tax treatment once your PTE is up and running.

First, if you own a PTE in one of the so-called "listed professions" forbidden from taking advantage of the 20% PTE deduction — whether as a sole owner or partner — you should book an appointment with a tax lawyer ASAP. The hacks I described in the previous section are real, and they could save you a ton of money.

Second, if you are a non-listed professional employee of a company — an engineer working for a power utility, for example, or a junior architect at a large practice — you should sit down with a tax adviser to see whether you'd be better off "quitting" your job and becoming a "consultant" to your old employer. If your current taxable income is less than $157,500 individual/$315,000 joint, you will save money on your taxes by going solo.

There is one caveat: Leaving permanent employment to become a PTE-based consultant means giving up corporate benefits like medical, dental and 401(k). But there are couple of reasons that might not be as big a problem as you might think:

1. Self-employed people can contribute up to 25% of their QBI into a SEP-IRA, traditional or Roth.

   The current annual cap is $54,000 a year; you're not limited to $5,500. That is a viable alternative to a 401(k) — especially since you can manage your IRA investments yourself, as I've described several times in *The Bauman Letter* reports about self-directed IRAs.

2. The Trump administration recently authorized the formation of independent health insurance associations, which are ideal for self-employed people. Once they are up and running, self-employed people will be able to form insurance pools with others in their situation and benefit from the same risk-spreading actuarial dynamics that produce lower insurance premiums for corporate health plans.

3. When you're self-employed, you're going to find that you can book many "personal" expenses to your business accounts. Your home office, your PC and laptop, your phone, a portion of your utilities — anything that you use for work can be written off as a business cost, at least in part.

   That means that although your overall cash flow may be the same as a self-employed PTE owner as it was when you were an employee, you're going to still have access to many things that you need — and enjoy a lower overall tax burden since they are deductible business expenses.

And don't forget … the new tax law eliminates all "miscellaneous deductions" — including the deduction for home office expenses for employees who work remotely.

That makes setting up as a PTE even more attractive, since all those expenses could be assigned to your business, reducing your taxable income and keeping you below the threshold to take the full 20% QBI deduction.

Conclusion

Though Republicans promised a simpler tax system, all these new loopholes are certain to keep the nation's CPAs and tax attorneys busy.

For many people, the opportunity to game the tax system this way will be irresistible. But if you're on the fence about it, consider this … you may have no choice.

Consider existing partnerships, for example. Each partner will have to figure out their individual values for qualified business income and qualified property to calculate their tax-deductible QBI … just to file their individual 1040s. They'll have to figure out their individual share of the unadjusted basis of the partnership's qualified property. Based on how the law is written, many tax experts think this includes everything from real estate to paperclips.

And they'll have to be able to document all of this to the IRS, if necessary.

So many of us are going to have to grapple with this new PTE tax regime even if we don't choose to take advantage of any new loopholes. The rules for PTEs — including the simplest LLCs and partnerships — have changed, and you're going to need help figuring them out.

It's not just an accounting issue, either. You're going to need advice.

Much of the actual practice of tax law is shaped by opinions issued by the IRS in the form of "private letters" and other rulings on how to interpret the tax code.

That code now has some radical new modifications. That means the IRS is going to spend the next few years reacting to the good-faith efforts of tax attorneys to interpret the new rules for their clients.

The IRS can't just throw the book at someone who adopts a particular strategy based on good-faith efforts to interpret the new law during the period when the IRS is trying to figure it all out.

That creates a window of opportunity for many of us ... one we should seize ... but with experienced expert advice.

To my mind, the most qualified tax attorney I know is Josh Bennett, who has worked with me and with my father Bob Bauman for many years.

Whether you are based in Florida or not, he's a great place to start if you think any of this is going to apply to you this year — voluntarily or not:

Josh N. Bennett, Esq.
PA 440 North Andrews Avenue
Fort Lauderdale, FL 33301
Tel.: (954) 779-1661
Mobile: (786) 202-5674
Email: josh@joshbennett.com
Website: www.joshbennett.com

INCOME SECRET NO. 14:

Collect $770 With a Property Tax "Circuit Breaker" Refund

When was the last time you paid your property tax, only to open your mailbox some time later to find a $770 refund check inside?

If you did, it wasn't a fluke. It meant you were a part of a Circuit Breaker program, a little-known, special tax credit for homeowners and renters in at least a dozen states and the District of Columbia.

Originally, this government initiative was intended to provide property tax relief for older homeowners and renters who met certain income and other requirements.

However, in many states (including Maryland, Michigan, New Jersey, Vermont, Wisconsin and West Virginia) homeowners of all ages are eligible for a Circuit Breaker refund — and in some state, renters too.

Here's how it works: Eligible property owners can claim a credit that is equal to the amount by which their property tax payments — including water and sewer charges — exceed 10% of their annual income.

Meanwhile, tenants can claim a credit of 25% if the rent they paid is more than 10% of their yearly income.

What's more, eligible taxpayers can file for the credit up to three years *retroactively*.

And that's not all — even people who don't typically file returns because they don't owe taxes can apply for the refund.

Massachusetts (along with Maine, Montana, New Mexico, Oklahoma, Rhode Island, D.C. and the aforementioned states) has a Circuit Breaker refund program. Out of the 86,000 taxpayers who took advantage of it in 2012, the average refund was $774.

Eligibility requirements may differ from state to state and are subject to change. However, recent rules in Massachusetts were that total income for single people could not exceed $55,000 ($69,000 for a head of the household) or $82,000 for a married couple. For homeowners, the assessed value of their primary residence could not be more than $700,000.

Some beneficiaries of the Circuit Breaker program use their refunds for necessities like food, medicine and utilities.

What would *you* do with an extra $774 in your pocket?

To see if your state offers a Circuit Breaker property tax refund, contact your local Department of Revenue or visit https://itep.org/category/property-taxes and select "State Policy" for more information.

INCOME SECRET NO. 15:

Let Your Pet Earn You Some Tax Deductions

When we welcome a pet into our homes, they are looked at as a source of companionship and entertainment. They bring warmth, love and laughter.

But did you know that they can also potentially bring some valuable tax deductions into your life, lowering your obligation to the IRS?

While it is not easy to claim your pet as a business expense, there are six avenues pet owners can potentially use to lower their taxes thanks to their beloved pet.

1. Eliminate Pests With Your Cat

If you use your cat to keep your business free of rats, mice and other vermin, you could potentially deduct costs associated with your cat. In one example, a court upheld a business expense deduction of $300 for cat food when a cat was used to deter snakes and rats from a family-owned junkyard.

In order to get the deduction, it's important that you convince the IRS that the cat is "ordinary and necessary." That means that using a cat must be "common and accepted in your trade or business." Furthermore, the cat must be "helpful and appropriate."

2. Guard Dog to Keep You Safe

The IRS might struggle to accept your cat is a necessary pest deterrent, but it has been more accepting in the past of guard dogs, particularly if a business is in a troubled neighborhood.

Keep in mind that size is key when convincing the IRS your pet is a guard dog. It's unlikely that your Yorkie is going to be believed as an effective guard dog.

If you are going to deduct expenses related to your guard dog, keep records of the dog's hours and work-related purpose. You could potentially deduct expenses such as dog food, training and veterinary bills on Schedule C.

3. Service Animals

Do you have a service animal to help with your medical needs? You might be able to use it as a deduction since medical expenses are tax deductible if you itemize.

The first step is to get a doctor's prescription for your service animal or at least some documentation proving that you require a service animal as a medical necessity.

In addition, keep any documentation that shows your pet was trained to meet your medical needs. The IRS doesn't consider an animal a "service animal" unless it's been trained and certified.

You can also include the costs of purchasing and training guide dogs for the blind or hearing impaired. This includes veterinary, food and grooming expenses.

4. Foster Pet Deductions

Fostering animals can earn you tax benefits for charitable contributions. You can claim any unreimbursed expenses related to fostering animals from qualified nonprofit organizations. These deductions can be listed on a Schedule A as charitable donations. These expenses could include pet food, supplies and veterinary bills.

5. Offset Hobby Income

Has your show dog won prize money? While the IRS is happy to take a chunk of your winnings, you could potentially get some of that back by claiming related expenses such as training, showing, etc.

If you receive a 1099 each year for your hobby income, you can additionally deduct expenses related to that the hobby up to the amount earned.

Unfortunately, taking this deduction can be complicated. This deduction is subject to a threshold of 2% of your adjusted gross income (AGI).

For example, let's said that your AGI is $100,000 and you made $1,000 from pet shows. However, you accumulated $3,000 in expenses.

You would be allowed to deduct only $1,000 of expenses since you're allowed to deduct only up to the amount of income earned.

In this case, the $1,000 is less than 2% of your AGI, so you actually lose $2,000 from the pet shows — and you still have to pay taxes on the $1,000 in income you earned.

6. Moving Expenses

Have you moved for a job? Since you're already deducting you moving expenses, you can also deduct the cost of shipping your household pets to your new home.

To get this deduction, the IRS requires that you must prove:

- Your move must be closely related to the start of your work.
- You have to pass the distance test.
- You have to pass the time test.

For example, your new workplace must be at least 50 miles farther from your old home than your old workplace was. Furthermore, you must work full time for 39 weeks or more during the first year after you relocate.

INCOME SECRET NO. 16:

Never Pay U.S. Taxes Again

It was good to be some place other than the land where I was born and raised. Maryland's Eastern Shore has its charms. But it just couldn't compete with what I was experiencing.

I was in a city built on the slopes of a stunningly beautiful mountain, surrounded by the sea on three sides. In 20 minutes, I could escape to fragrant forests cut by cool streams flowing from the mountain above. The air was always crystal clear, thanks to the steady ocean breeze. A few hours' drive to the north, and I'd be in a gorgeous desert. Head east, and I'd find farmland and wineries that remind everyone who visit them of southern France.

The locals were friendly — not unlike the rough-edged but good-natured kids I'd known back in Maryland. They liked to drink a bit of beer, enjoy sunshine and waves, and check out live music in the city's numerous pubs. I made friends quickly and easily. I met a gorgeous girlfriend.

After a few months, I landed a nice job teaching at the city's world-class university, also built on the slopes of the mountain. I was a student as well, but the local tertiary education system was built around a "tutorial" system that generated a constant demand for tutors. It paid my tuition and then some.

After my first year, I was promoted to lecturer. By year three, I had been recruited by a top-notch economic research team to develop proposals for the country's manufacturing sector.

One thing led to another, and by year five I was a senior executive at a nonprofit financial institution with a great salary, a permanent resident and had settled in for good. I had acquired a home in a quaint seaside village. I fell asleep to the sound of Indian Ocean surf.

And for the whole time, I didn't pay a dime in U.S. income tax.

Many of you have probably heard that there's a way you can pay no U.S. tax on a certain amount of your household income. In fact, it's probably the single most popular topic with new subscribers to *The Bauman Letter*. People want to know how this works … and for good reason! Who likes paying taxes?

It's not a hoax. Under certain circumstances, you can pay no U.S. tax on a portion of your income. After all, I did this for more than 20 years. It's something called the foreign earned income exclusion (FEIE). It allows you to exempt — completely — a certain portion of your annual earnings from U.S. tax. You report the income, but you just don't owe any tax on it.

The FEIE is the reason I didn't pay any U.S. income tax from 1985 to 2007. I paid South African income tax, of course, but it was much lower than U.S. rates.

That meant I could save more and acquire a car, a house and other essential capital goods much more quickly than if I'd stayed in the U.S. Which I duly did.

You don't have to go as far as Cape Town to benefit from the FEIE. It's not for everyone, but it does provide a major incentive to move offshore. And when combined with the right business strategy, it can save you huge amounts in tax over your lifetime.

Let me tell you how.

The Strange Logic of U.S. Taxation

To understand the foreign earned income exclusion, you need to understand the way the U.S. government thinks about us, as citizens and taxpayers. It's not how most governments think.

That's for sure.

Most sensible countries only tax income earned within their own borders. There are exceptions, of course, but as a rule, most countries use a "territorial" tax system. This is based on the sensible logic that your earnings from the national economy are a proxy for your consumption of that economy's "public goods," like roads, policing, courts, defense and so on. If you're not earning money inside the country, you're assumed not to be consuming those goods — at least, not as much of them. Hence, no taxes on foreign income.

The U.S. government — by pretty much full bipartisan agreement — takes the opposite course. Unlike most other countries, our tax system doesn't end at our borders. Instead, we Americans are taxed on our global income, no matter where we earn it or where we live. This is known as a worldwide tax system.

I never could figure out why the U.S. does this. My best guess is that two American peculiarities are at work.

First, Americans — government and citizens alike — tend to see the country as exceptional, a unique case in the world. We're so powerful, and there are so many benefits to being a U.S. citizen, that it's a bargain, not a burden, to be taxed on our global income.

We should gladly contribute to our glorious tax authorities, so the U.S. can continue the important work of being great and powerful. After all, so many foreigners want to live here!

Second, Americans living or working abroad come from many different states and congressional districts. There's no U.S. jurisdiction where there are so many U.S. voters living abroad that it would be worth a congressman's time to introduce and push a bill to change the worldwide tax system for Americans living abroad.

If they did, moreover, political opponents would scream bloody murder, claiming that "foreign Americans" were getting special treatment.

Whatever the reasons, when it comes to U.S. taxes, there's no essential difference between living in the U.S. and living abroad. American "persons" (i.e., a U.S. taxpayer, whether citizen or green card holder) living abroad must still report all their income, file their returns and pay their income taxes to the IRS.

As you may imagine, that poses a problem ... and creates an opportunity for you. There are a lot of American "persons" working abroad. They pay taxes to the countries where they work (unless they work for an American firm or the U.S. government, in which case they pay the IRS).

If the U.S. taxes them too, they're gonna be major league unhappy — as will foreign employers and governments that benefit from their work.

The solution, practiced by most countries in the world today, is what's known as a double-taxation agreement, or DTA.

DTAs aim to eliminate the taxation of income by more than one country. The U.S. has dozens of such agreements covering all major economies. They allow the country where the income arises to deduct income tax through their own withholding systems and require the IRS to grant the U.S. person taxed by them to receive a compensating foreign tax credit on their U.S. tax return.

The same applies in reverse for foreign taxpayers in the U.S. That way everyone ends up paying what they would pay if they were working in their own country — unless, of course, the income tax rates between the two are very different.

To make DTAs work, however, the two taxation authorities must exchange information. That requires time and effort. In a rare instance of common sense, Congress decided that income earned by certain U.S. persons abroad below a cutoff would be exempted from U.S. income tax entirely ... because anything less than that just isn't worth pursuing.

Tax-Free Income ... Literally

Double-taxation agreements are the reason we have the foreign earned income exclusion.

The FEIE is essentially an admission that it's not worth the U.S. government's time and effort to reconcile tax records for individual filers earning under a certain amount. As odd as it may seem to us, the cost of pursuing tax on roughly $100,000 in annual foreign income cancels out the benefit.

Exempting such income saves the IRS lots of hassle over nothing ... and presents an opportunity for us.

The desire for tax efficiency also explains why the FEIE isn't a tax credit. It's a tax exemption.

Under the FEIE, the IRS literally exempts the first $102,100 of your foreign income from U.S. federal income tax.

For a two-person household of U.S. persons where both are working, the amount is double — $204,200. The FEIE is indexed annually for inflation and so increases every year.

In other words, if you qualify for the FEIE for 2017, and you earn $102,100 or less in wages, you will pay zero federal income taxes — zip, nada. You still must file your 1040 and some other forms, but you'll owe no tax.

Examples

1. Fred and Joyce, in their mid-60s, retired to a Central American country that has a tax treaty with the U.S. They sold their U.S. home and closed their U.S. business, investing the proceeds in a mix of U.S. and offshore financial vehicles.

   They planned to live on the proceeds of these investments and annuities, which would be transferred to their accounts in their new home country as needed. Before long, Fred began to get requests from local businesses for help in his areas of expertise.

   Unable to resist the lure of a little extra income, he began to oblige. Joyce also began to make and sell craft goods in local markets.

   Fred and Joyce pay U.S. tax on their U.S.-based investment income, receive U.S. tax credits for investment taxes paid in foreign countries, and pay no U.S. tax on their limited local earnings, since they qualify for the FEIE.

2. Rob decided to give life in the Mediterranean a try. The island nation where he hoped to settle didn't tax his investment income from the U.S., so he left it in U.S. investments for the first year.

Once he decided to buy a home and stay, he transferred most of his U.S. capital to investments in his new home country, since the tax rate on his earnings was much lower than in the U.S., as were the brokerage fees.

He no longer pays U.S. taxes on these offshore investments and receives a credit on his U.S. taxes for the taxes he does pay on these now foreign investment earnings.

If you earn more than $102,100, however, you'll be liable for U.S. income tax on the excess. For example, if you earn $202,100 in salary, you will pay U.S. federal income tax on $100,000 at 28% to 33%.

Note that even with the FEIE, your tax bracket is determined by your full earnings of $202,100. You are paying a rate on your last $100,000 as if you had earned $202,100 in wages, not just $100,000.

The FEIE exempts the first $102,100 from tax, but it doesn't change your overall tax bracket. If you pay tax in the country where you work, however, your U.S. tax on this $100,000 over and above the FEIE will be reduced: Every dollar you pay in foreign income tax should reduce your U.S. tax by one dollar.

Catch No. 1: You Must Leave

The FEIE is there for the taking. But it does come with a cost … at least, depending on your definition of cost.

You see, to qualify for the FEIE, you must be:

a. Physically out of the U.S. for 330 days during any 12-month period, or…

b. A legal resident of a foreign country for a full calendar year, and…

c. Earning foreign source income from employment or a business.

The 330-day test is simple math. It doesn't matter where you are in the world, so long as you're not in the U.S. You don't have to be a resident of any other country. You just can't be in the U.S.

That's what some folks call being a "perpetual traveler." If you are traveling physically outside the U.S. for 330 days out of 12 months, you qualify for the FEIE on your foreign income, even if you are using temporary visitor visas abroad and don't acquire residence anywhere other than the U.S.

I know a few folks who do this. For example, one guy I know spends three to four months each year in a variety of different countries. He owns homes in some of them and uses hotels or stays with friends in others. His income comes from a publishing business registered in a tax-free jurisdiction.

All the income earned by that foreign business is considered foreign-sourced, even if it results from sales in the U.S. itself, because it is first booked to the foreign business, which then pays him a salary that is covered by the FEIE.

The residence test is more complex. It's based on your "intentions." This test involves moving to a foreign country for the "foreseeable future" and making it both your home and your home base — i.e., it's where you return when you travel. For that reason, it also must be a place where you're a legal permanent resident, with a residence permit or passport.

Finally, you must follow the country's tax laws as a legal resident, paying taxes if they are levied on income.

The residence test has one major advantage over the 330-day rule: It allows you to spend more time in the U.S. Under the

330-day test, you can spend a maximum of 36 days a year here. If you qualify for the residency test, you can spend four or five months a year in the U.S.

But remember that any income earned directly in the U.S. by you personally is taxable — the FEIE doesn't apply to U.S.-sourced income. If you work for 10 days in the U.S., the income from those days counts as a U.S. source of income and will be taxed.

As I've already noted, I'm a perfect example of residence-test FEIE. From 1985 to 2007, all my income from employment and self-employment was foreign-sourced. Most of it was in South Africa, but I also received contract income from international agencies based in Europe.

From 1985 to 1990, I was a legal resident of South Africa on a student visa. After that, I became a permanent resident. In 2002, I became a South African citizen. The whole time I paid South African income tax. My income never exceeded the FEIE limits, so I paid no U.S. income tax at all.

Catch No. 2: Unearned Income

The FEIE doesn't apply to income that's not "earned."

"Earned" income is money made in the current period from employment or a business.

"Unearned" income is passive income such as dividends, interest, capital gains, alimony, pensions, annuities and Social Security benefits. It's called that because you really earned this income years ago, but deferred using it until now.

In many cases, you may receive unearned income from a variety of sources around the world. The typical U.S. retiree abroad, for example, will receive a variety of unearned income, including Social Security, corporate pensions, private pensions, annuities and dividends on investments.

In most cases, this unearned income will be taxed exactly as if you lived in the U.S. Any U.S.-sourced investment income you receive, even if it is paid out abroad, will be taxed by the IRS just as if you were living here, at U.S. rates.

For example, if you live in Mexico on the proceeds of U.S. investments and Social Security, you'll report, file and pay tax on that income just as if you were living in the U.S. itself.

On the other hand, any foreign-source unearned income you receive — such as dividends or interest — will be taxed per the laws of the country where the investment resides, at their tax rates. As I explained above, in most cases that foreign tax can be taken as a credit on your U.S. taxes.

For example, if you live in Mexico on the proceeds of investments located in Switzerland, you will pay tax to the Swiss government as per their laws. Any Swiss tax you pay can be deducted from your U.S. tax obligations, so you pay the same tax you would as if you received all your income in the U.S. itself.

Catch No. 3: Tax Rates Matter

One critical thing to understand about the FEIE is that only people living in low-tax countries will get much benefit.

If you are based in a place with a tax rate that is the same or higher than the U.S., then the foreign tax credit will prevent double taxation, without the need for the FEIE.

For example, if your U.S. federal tax rate is 35%, and your rate in France is 40%, you don't need the FEIE because you are already paying more in French tax than you would in the U.S. You can deduct your French tax on your U.S. tax return without concerning yourself with qualifying for the FEIE. Of course, you will end up paying more tax overall because the French rate is higher.

Conversely, if you are living tax-free in a place like Panama, drawing a salary of $100,000 and fail to qualify for the FEIE, 100% of your income is taxable in the U.S. Without the FEIE, there is no benefit to working in a low-tax country.

The Big Opportunity: The Offshore Business Loophole

The FEIE creates one of the greatest tax plays I know. Here's how it works.

Let's say you operate a small business through an offshore corporation. You pay yourself a salary up to $102,100. That makes it eligible for the FEIE. If spouses are both operating the business, they can draw a combined $204,200 and leave the rest of the money in the corporation.

But what if your net profits exceed the FEIE amount? What if you earn $1 million? Must you pay U.S. tax on $897,800? Yes … unless you structure your business to provide for retained earnings in your offshore corporation.

If you do that, you can shield those retained profits from U.S. tax until you decide to draw them down … including in the form of an FEIE-compliant future salary, making them tax-free.

In other words, if you take more than the FEIE out of the corporation as salary, you will pay tax on the excess as earned income. But if you leave the excess in the corporation's accounts, it will be classified as retained earnings and won't be taxable by the U.S. until it's distributed as a dividend.

It may even be possible to pay out retained earnings as FEIE-qualifying salary in future years, as long as the business is still in operation, and you can demonstrate a legitimate business need to pay salaries from retained earnings rather than current revenue. If you can't, it's considered a dividend and is taxable unearned income.

Bear in mind, as I noted above, that all this assumes you are living and working in a jurisdiction that levies no or low income taxes on the $102,100 that you draw as salary. If you're trying to do this in France, where the tax rate is 40%, you're not going to save anything … in fact, you'll pay more.

There are two important caveats to this trick. First, interest or capital gains on the retained earnings may be taxable, depending on the jurisdiction. Second, you may not borrow retained earnings or use them for your personal benefit. They must remain in the corporation.

So, what counts as a "properly structured offshore corporation"?

1. It must be a corporation — not a limited liability company (LLC), foundation, partnership or other pass-through entity. In other words, it must have a separate tax and legal identify from you.

2. It must be incorporated in a country that will not tax your profits. Otherwise, there is no point.

3. Retained earnings must arise from ordinary business income — income received from the sale of a product attributable to the normal and recurring operations of the company. You can't just book profits from other activities through a corporate shell.

   The product doesn't have to be physical; it is possible, for example, to sell your writings via a foreign corporation as a product. There are limits to this, as I'll show below.

4. You must report your activities and retained earnings of the offshore corporation on IRS Form 5471, report the corporation's foreign bank account under FATCA and keep up on all other U.S. reporting requirements.

One tricky aspect of this corporate loophole is the notion of an "ordinary business." Yours must be an ordinary business to qualify for the tax deferral on retained earnings. The definition of an ordinary business has two parts:

First, you must sell something on a regular and continuous basis; you should make a profit in at least three of the last five years; you should work at the enterprise full-time; and it must be a business, not a hobby.

Second, you should be selling a product, not providing a professional service such as consulting.

Now, it can be hard to determine where consulting ends and selling a "product" begins; this is where getting good legal advice is essential.

But if you are deemed by the IRS to be operating a consulting or professional service business, you may utilize the FEIE, but you are not allowed to hold retained earnings in your offshore corporation.

Other Useful Facts

1. The FEIE doesn't apply to self-employment tax (FICA), only income tax. A self-employed person living abroad and qualifying for the FEIE will still pay 15% in self-employment tax, i.e., $15,330 on a FEIE-qualifying income of $102,100.

2. Unearned passive income from interest, dividends and investments isn't active income and thus doesn't qualify for the FEIE. Unearned passive income flows through to you as shareholder of the foreign corporation and is taxable on your personal 1040 return.

   However, you can elect to pay U.S. tax on the appreciation in your corporate account each year, or you can pay U.S. tax on the gain when you sell funds or shares from your account. If you elect to pay tax when you sell, however, a punitive interest rate is added to the tax due to eliminate any benefit from deferral.

3. An offshore corporation may have shareholders who live in the United States. These shareholders must be passive investors who have no control over the company's day-to-day operations. The offshore corporation should not have a U.S. office or employees, or any U.S. agents working exclusively to market or distribute its goods in the U.S.

Reporting

Remember that you must file U.S. tax returns regardless of your FEIE status. I filed every year for two decades in South Africa without paying any U.S. taxes.

If you go the offshore business route, you must maintain records of income and expense in accordance with U.S. accounting principles. Offshore corporations must file many U.S. tax forms, under threat of major penalties:

- Form 5471 — Information Return of U.S. Persons With Respect to Certain Foreign Corporations (http://www.irs. gov/pub/irs-pdf/f5471.pdf).

- Form 926 — Report of Transfer to Foreign Company, filed when you fund the offshore corporation (http://www.irs. gov/pub/irs-pdf/f926.pdf).

- FBAR — Financial Crimes Enforcement Network (FinCEN) 114, Report of Foreign Bank and Financial Accounts (https://www.irs.gov/businesses/small-businesses-self-employed/report-of-foreign-bank-and-financial-accounts-fbar).

- A foreign corporation or limited liability company must make an election to be treated as a corporation, partnership or disregarded entity using default classifications in Form 8832, Entity Classification Election (http://www.irs. gov/pub/irs-pdf/f8832.pdf).

- Form 8858 — Information Return of U.S. Persons With Respect to Foreign Disregarded Entities (http://www.irs. gov/pub/irs-pdf/f8858.pdf).

- Form 5472 — Information Return of a 25% Foreign-Owned U.S. Corporation (http://www.irs.gov/pub/irs-pdf/f5472. pdf).

- Form 8938 — FATCA (https://www.irs.gov/pub/irs-pdf/ f8938.pdf). This applies to your personal accounts as well as the accounts of any corporate entity you control.

Conclusion: Not a DIY Matter

One thing that should be clear by now is that although FEIE can be simple — as it was for me in South Africa — it can quickly become very complicated indeed, especially if you opt to form an offshore corporation.

That's why I strongly recommend that you engage qualified, experienced tax counsel if and when you decide to eliminate taxes by moving abroad. Here are some of the key things to consider:

- An expatriate's tax return is more complicated than a normal U.S. tax return. That should be clear from what I've said here.

- You may have to reconcile your host-country tax year to the U.S. tax year. The U.S. tax year begins on January 1 and ends on December 31. Not all countries operate on this calendar. For example, Australia, Hong Kong, New Zealand and the U.K. all have different tax-year schedules that don't coincide with the calendar year.

- The IRS requires that you (or your tax preparer) prepare your return per the U.S. tax year, which means taking your tax statements from your host country for two years, extracting the appropriate information and then plugging it into your U.S. tax return.

- You must keep up with all changes in U.S. tax rules and legislation from afar. The U.S. tax code changes every year, especially when there are major changes in the political landscape. If you're not a tax professional, you probably don't have the time or inclination to keep up with these changes.

- You may be required to file a state return, even if you have not lived in the U.S. for a few years. Every U.S. state has its own rules, and certain states make it more difficult to avoid filing their tax return. You may have a state tax domicile if you maintain a state driver's license, state voter registration or bank accounts or property in that state.

- Commercial tax software isn't designed with expats in mind and may miss deductions or exclusions that could cost you money. You may save a few dollars upfront by using them, but you could end up losing a significant amount in overpaid taxes or missed credits in the long run.

My go-to guy on these matters is my good friend Josh Bennett. He specializes in the intersection between U.S. and foreign tax and corporate rules. He can be reached as follows:

Josh N. Bennett, Esq.
440 North Andrews Avenue
Fort Lauderdale, FL 33301
Tel.: 1-954-779-1661
Mobile: 1-786-202-5674
Email: josh@joshbennett.com
Website: www.joshbennett.com

RETIREMENT

A recent Gallup poll revealed that roughly 49% of people don't expect to have saved enough money to live comfortably in retirement. Americans already have a poor track record when it comes to saving and when you throw in the multiple options available for retirement planning, many are simply too overwhelmed. In this section, there are tricks for boosting your Social Security payments, how to choose between a traditional IRA and a Roth IRA, and even how you can boost your retirement investment options by opening a self-directed IRA. Learn the steps you need to take to maximize your retirement savings.

INCOME SECRET NO. 17:

Boost Your Social Security Benefit by Retiring *Earlier*

Social Security is a huge entitlement program that shells out more than $950 billion in benefits annually to about 67 million Americans. Most beneficiaries derive 50 percent or more of their retirement income from the program, while 21% of married recipients and 43% of unmarried individuals depend on it for 90% or more of their income.

You spend your working years contributing to the program, so why not try to get as much income out of the program in retirement as you can? After all, isn't that what Social Security is for?

Well, if you think the Social Security Administration is looking out for your best interest by encouraging you to delay drawing your benefits until your age 70, you may want to reconsider that assumption.

At first glance, this might seem like a good idea since your benefits at 70 will be 32% higher than those you would receive at age 62. However, contrary to popular belief, you stand to make *more money* by taking your benefits as early as possible.

How can that be?

As you probably know, 62 is the earliest age you can start collecting your Social Security retirement benefits, but you earn delayed retirement credits equal to 8% per year plus inflation for every year you delay claiming benefits past full retirement age, which is 66 for people born between 1943 and 1954, and 67 for those born after 1960.

On the next page is a table showing how much smaller your benefits will be if you elect to collect them before you reach your full retirement age:

Start Collecting At:	Full Retirement Age of 65	Full Retirement Age of 66	Full Retirement Age of 67
62	80%	75%	70%
63	86.7%	80%	75%
64	93.3%	86.7%	80%
65	100%	93.3%	86.7%
66		100%	93.3%
67			100%
(Data source: Social Security Administration)			

It would appear from that table that you'd be better off waiting until your full retirement age to collect Social Security. But there's a factor you must consider — namely, how long do you intend to live?

You see, the Social Security system is designed in such a way that if you live an average length time, your total benefits received will be more or less the same regardless of when you start collecting them. Payments that begin at age 62 will be substantially smaller, but you'll receive many more of them. So whether you live a little longer or shorter than average, there isn't that much difference.

Nevertheless, many Americans refrain from claiming Social Security benefits as soon as they reach 62 because they've been told that the longer they wait, the more they will be paid — which is true on a short-term basis. But since the average U.S. lifespan is 78, you're more likely to lose money in the long run by waiting.

True, if you live a little longer or shorter than average, your total benefits received will not be vastly different whether you start collecting at age 62 or age 70. And if longevity runs in your family and you can keep working longer, waiting might make more sense. But why gamble on living a very long life, if you can start enjoying that retirement income now?

Besides, the sooner you start collecting Social Security benefits, the more money you'll receive in the long run. Consider this:

A 50-year old who earns $60,000 annually stands to make $199,212 by age 75 if he or she retires at 62, versus $145,140 from retiring at 70. That's $54,072 more in Social Security benefits!

Of course, not everyone can afford to retire at age 62. It depends on how much money you'll need to live comfortably for the rest of your life. Social Security is just one source of income — and not a lucrative one at that.

The average monthly retirement benefit was recently $1,371, amounting to $16,452 per year, while the overall maximum monthly Social Security benefit for those retiring at their full retirement age in 2017 is $2,687 — or roughly $32,000 for the whole year. Those who retire at age 70 in 2017 can collect monthly checks as large as $3,538, for $42,456 per year — though most people will receive less.

To find out what *you* can expect to receive from Social Security, go to www.ssa.gov, and set up a "my Social Security" account. It will provide you with information on your estimated benefits. Even if the numbers don't seem all that impressive, you may still be able to retire early depending on how far from retirement you are. Why? Because your money is growing at an annual average rate of 8%, as illustrated in the following table.

Growing at 8% For:	$10,000 Invested Annually	$15,000 Invested Annually	$20,000 Invested Annually
3 years	$35,061	$52,592	$70,122
5 years	$63,359	$95,039	$126,719
10 years	$156,455	$234,682	$312,910
15 years	$293,243	$439,864	$586,486
20 years	$494,229	$741,344	$988,458
25 years	$789,544	$1.2 million	$1.6 million

But even if you take longevity out of the equation, there may be other good reasons to start collecting Social Security early:

- **So you can retire earlier.** Early retirement means you can enjoy your money while you're still relatively young, healthy, active and able to travel. Provided, of course, you have other savings or sources of income. Note, however, if you take your benefits before your full retirement age, you'll be taxed for your benefits if you are still employed, depending on how much you earn.

- **You're married and want to take advantage of an overall spousal strategy.** If you and your spouse have very different earnings records, you might start collecting the benefits of the spouse with the lower lifetime earnings record early, while delaying the start of collecting the benefits of the higher-earning spouse. That way, you both get to enjoy some income earlier, and when the higher earner hits 70, you can collect their extra-large checks. Also, should that higher-earning spouse die first, the spouse with the smaller earnings history can collect those bigger benefit checks.

- **You have no choice but to retire early.** Sometimes, you aren't the one who gets to decide when to retire — your circumstances choose it for you. Some retirees are forced to leave the workforce sooner than they planned due to health problems or a disability. Others corporate downsizing or because their company went out of business. In those situations, having Social Security benefits available sooner rather than later provides a relative modest, but nevertheless welcome safety net.

This is just one of several hidden strategies to boost your Social Security income. In the next Income Secret, we'll show you how you can significantly increase your income by NOT filing for two types of Social Security benefits simultaneously.

INCOME SECRET NO. 18:

How to Collect an Extra $5,600 per Year in Social Security Benefits

Marriage certainly has its perks — love, companionship, emotional support ... and potentially extra Social Security benefits.

There are numerous strategies that enable married couples to maximize their benefits by coordinating the timing of their claims.

For example, they have the option of claiming benefits based on their own earnings or choose to receive up to 50% of the amount for which their spouse is eligible at full retirement age. This game plan can provide an important safety net for parents who stayed out of the workforce for an extended period of time in order to care for their children.

There is also the strategy of claiming twice. Dual-earner couples who have reached their full retirement age may be able to claim spousal benefits and then later switch to payments based on their own work record, which will then be higher due to delayed claiming. That way, if you're planning to delay drawing benefits until age 70, you can receive some benefit between age 66 and 70.

However, there is another marriage-related income booster that stands out among the rest — and it comes right out of the Social Security Administration's public documents but is buried amid so much other confusing information that many retirees completely miss out on it.

It enables you to collect an extra $5,600 in Social Security benefits each year by filling out two forms instead of one. The trick, however, is to NOT file for two types of Social Security benefits simultaneously, but rather to file for one (typically the smaller on) at 62, then wait until age 66 and file for the other.

If you're eligible for a retirement benefit and a survivor benefit, for example, you'll lose out on one if you file for both simultaneously. That's because, under Social Security rules, you can only collect the larger of the two. The better strategy is to take the smaller benefit first, then claim the larger one later.

Here's an example: Edith is a 62-year-old widow. She lost her husband before he could claim any Social Security benefits. At her age, Edith is eligible for her own monthly retirement benefit ($1,800) and a survivor benefit ($2,000). But if she claims both at once, she'd only receive a check for $2,000 a month for the rest of her life.

Edith would do better to claim her retirement benefit at 62, and wait until age 66 — her full retirement age — to claim her survivor benefit, which will now equal what would have been her husband's benefit at his full retirement age — $2,469. That way, she'd get $1,800 a month for four years (from 62 to 66), then $2,469 a month for the rest of her life.

That's a 23% higher real benefit from age 66 to her death, than had she settled for the $2,000 a month survivor benefit. It means that Edith would pocket an extra $5,628 per year.

With that higher payment, it would take Edith less than two years to make back the $200 a month she forfeited from ages 62 to 66.

Not only that, but let's say Edith lives at least another 20 years (to age 86). That's approximately $5,600 per year times 20 equals $112,000 in extra benefits ... not including Social Security cost-of-living adjustments.

You've already discovered two ways to significantly boost your Social Security income. Next, however, you'll learn how to potentially score the biggest payoff of all...

INCOME SECRET NO. 19:

Boost Your Social Security Benefits by $1,140 per Month ... or More

Rules are funny things — especially when they pertain to government entitlement programs.

For example, just because you've elected to take your Social Security benefits at an earlier age — say, 62 — doesn't mean you're locked into collecting only the minimum monthly allowance due to you. Not when there's an often-overlooked Social Security "reset" rule that can boost your benefits by a whopping $1,140 per month.

Let's say you jumped at the opportunity to claim Social Security benefits when you reached 62, but now realize that you don't need this source of income just yet.

Or perhaps you changed your mind about retiring and decided instead to continue working.

Or maybe you just have beneficiary's remorse and wish you would have waited until you reached your full retirement age — or even 70 — to take advantage of your Social Security benefits.

Well, you can. You're entitled to a "do-over" and can actually postpone collecting benefits until you're older. In fact, making such a move could be the difference between collecting only $1,277 per month at age 62 and getting $2,419 per month at age 70.

Perhaps financial need was behind your initial decision to take those early benefits. Or maybe you were worried about the long-term viability of the Social Security program, which many have warned will go bankrupt within the next two decades. Regardless of the reason, the consequences of taking early Social Security benefits can be significant.

If your full retirement age is 66 and you start taking payments at 62, it would result in a permanent 25% reduction in benefits. Put another way, if your full retirement age (FRA) benefit was expected to be $2,000 per month, electing to collect benefits at age 62 would reduce that amount to $1,500 per month. It would produce a shortfall that — when you take into consideration that Social Security benefits are indexed for inflation — would add up to thousands of dollars in lost income.

But there is a way to mitigate such a decision after the fact, and it's perfectly in compliance with Social Security rules.

Upon reaching full retirement age, you can stop receiving benefits until later in the future. In the meantime, under the program rules, delayed benefits after full retirement age are entitled to earn credits of 8% per year up to age 70. Which means that if your FRA is 66 and you delay your benefits until you reach age 70, you will receive delayed credits totaling up to 32% (or 132% of your primary insurance amount (PIA) as shown in the chart below).

Age when you claim retirement benefits	Amount of retirement benefit
5 years before FRA	70% of PIA
4 years before FRA	75% of PIA
3 years before FRA	80% of PIA
2 years before FRA	86.67% of PIA
1 year before FRA	93.33% of PIA
at FRA	100% of PIA
1 year after FRA	108% of PIA
2 years after FRA	116% of PIA
3 years after FRA	124% of PIA
4 years after FRA	132% of PIA

Here's an example of this strategy...

John was gainfully employed up until he lost his job at age 62. Unable to find other work, he decided it best to just retire and live off his savings, a modest pension and his Social Security benefits. Had he waited until his full retirement age of 66, John's monthly Social Security benefits would have been about $2,000. Instead, it was reduced to $1,500 (or 75% of what he would have collected at age 66) due to his decision to take an early benefit.

However, John belatedly learns about this "reset" rule. So, when he reaches his full retirement age of 66, he decides to suspend his benefit until age 70. This benefit now starts earning delayed credits at a rate of 8% per year. Which means that at age 70 (four years after his full retirement age), he will be entitled to 132% of his PIA.

So, when John resumes taking his benefit at age 70, he recovers 99% of the original primary insurance amount (0.75 times 1.32 equals 0.99) and receives $1,980 per month for the rest of his life, along with any inflation adjustments.

Of course, had John originally delayed taking his benefit until age 70 (four years beyond his FRA), it would have increased to $2,640 per month with delayed credits ($2,000 times 1.32 equals $2,640). Nevertheless, by suspending his benefit for a time, he has considerably improved his financial circumstances despite his prior decision to take an early benefit.

Thanks to the "reset" option allowing suspension of Social Security benefits at full retirement age, many beneficiaries can not only undo the impact of having taken early benefits, but also significantly boost their monthly and yearly income to meet their spending needs throughout retirement.

In fact, doing so could be one of the best "secret" income moves you'll ever make.

To apply, simply fill out the SSA-521 form within 12 months of becoming entitled to your retirement benefits. You are limited to one withdrawal. For more details on applying for a "do-over", visit https://www.ssa.gov/planners/retire/withdrawal.html.

INCOME SECRET NO. 20:

Roth or Traditional IRA: Don't Let
Taxes Eat Into Your Retirement

Quick: How do you set your annual retirement savings goal?

Very wealthy households usually seek professional assistance. Once you get to the point where planning for estate tax is an issue — when you and your spouse expect to leave more than $11 million in gross estate — it's indispensable, since you must juggle multiple types of tax.

But if you're like most people, you base your savings on a combination of IRS contribution limits (for IRAs), 401(k) employer matches (if you're employed) and rules of thumb, such as 10% of pretax income.

A recent study found that most American retirement savers do exactly that. They let the system decide for them how much to save based on the tax rules and their employers' whims.

That's understandable. But the interesting fact is that they do so regardless of the type of savings vehicle they use ... with remarkable results ... results that provide a fascinating free lesson in retirement planning.

To Roth or Not to Roth: That Is the Question

Individual retirement accounts (IRAs) and 401(k) plans come in two flavors: traditional and Roth. Contributions to the former are tax-exempt — i.e., you don't pay tax on the income you set aside for them. Your accumulated contributions plus investment growth are taxed when you withdraw them in retirement.

Since the IRS gave you a tax break when you saved into a traditional vehicle, it insists on its pound of flesh when you retire in the form of annual required minimum distributions (RMDs). Those can create massive headaches and tax complications for retirees.

Contributions to a Roth vehicle, on the other hand, are subject to tax … but the proceeds are tax-free when you retire — and there are no RMDs.

At the level of logic and math, the decision to go the traditional or Roth route should depend on a combination of your cash flow needs during your working life and your expectation of future tax rates.

All else being equal, if you need more money now and/or expect taxes to remain the same or fall in the future, you'd go the traditional route. If you can spare the extra tax now and/or expect tax rates to rise in the future, you'd choose Roth. That's because if you expect future taxes to be higher, it makes sense to pay them now when they're low.

Dumb Luck

In 2018, a married couple filing jointly can contribute a maximum of $11,000 to their IRAs, whether Roth or traditional. Contributing to a traditional IRA lowers their current tax bill; they'll pay later. Contributing to a Roth leaves it unchanged, but future withdrawals are tax-free.

In theory, that sets up a complex net present value calculation of current versus future income, tax rate expectations and other factors.

But most Americans don't think about that. They contribute the same amount whether it's to a traditional or Roth vehicle. As Harvard Business School researchers found, that's because they simply save according to the IRS maximum, whether it's a traditional or Roth IRA.

If they have a Roth IRA, this accidental choice creates a huge unintended retirement windfall.

Let's say the couple saved $5,000 a year in an IRA for 40 years, earning a 5% annual return. Their balance at retirement will be more than $600,000.

If the IRA is a Roth, the full balance is available for their retirement spending. If it's traditional, taxes are due on the balance.

Let's say their tax rate is 20% in retirement. That's what they'll pay on withdrawals from their traditional IRA — which they must take whether they need them or not, due to the RMD rules.

If they opt for a Roth, on the other hand, their taxes will already have been paid, and they'll enjoy $120,000 extra spending power in retirement — about $700 a month more.

A No-Brainer

I've said it before, and I'll say it again: U.S. income tax rates will be higher in the future. That makes a Roth IRA a more sensible choice.

Our current income tax rates are the lowest in over a century. Our national debt is enormous and growing. Those in charge of the federal government show no signs of reining it in — quite the opposite. The population is ageing, but retirement benefits are politically sacrosanct. Our national infrastructure requires urgent and expensive repairs. And so on.

When taxes do go up, having a Roth IRA and/or 401(k) means you'll be able to ignore them. Some people will be in that situation accidentally.

You, on the other hand, can choose it consciously. My advice is to do so … it's a no-brainer.

INCOME SECRET NO. 21:

Why the Self-Directed IRA is Your Key to Long-Term Prosperity

I'm a do-it-yourself (DIY) sort of guy. It's taught me something I want to share with you.

In my personal life, my research and writing, I'm biased toward solutions that give me maximum choice and control. I like to service my own motorbike. I do my own basic electrical repairs and plumbing. I file my own taxes ... unless they get really complicated, in which case I know where to draw the line and bring in an expert. DIY doesn't mean do it alone.

I've learned — often the hard way — that trusting big, remote institutions to make decisions or do things for me is asking for trouble. Retirement planning is an excellent case in point.

For a few years I had a 403(b) plan from a previous employer. It offered a fixed range of investment options. Some of them were superficially attractive, but once I took into account plan fees and the costs associated with specific funds, it became clear that I'd do better by ending my participation in the plan, paying tax on the compensation that would have gone to contributions, and investing it myself.

That's why I now manage my own retirement funds ... with the help of the right experts.

The fact is that most garden-variety institutional retirement plans — including individual retirement accounts (IRAs) — are designed to gather people's retirement savings and direct them to U.S. stock markets. An entire "food chain" has grown up around the U.S. retirement system, that more or less guarantees that you won't do any better than inflation, even if the underlying investments occasionally do.

But the biggest problem with conventional retirement plans is a lack of investment options. Why should you have to limit yourself to someone else's choices, made for their own convenience and profit? You don't. You don't have to limit yourself to dollar-based U.S. equities and bonds. You can pursue almost any investment option imaginable … real estate, business start-ups, intellectual property, precious metals … you name it.

You want more for your IRA. And you can have it … a lot more.

Take Control of Your Future … and Your Present

There's about $17.5 trillion in all U.S. private pensions. More than 25% of it in personal IRAs. For a clever few, some of that money is in "self-directed" IRAs … about 2% of the total. Those are the folks who have found that a more flexible approach to retirement planning provides the best returns and asset protection.

A self-directed IRA is a critical tool, regardless of how DIY you are. It's legal, profitable and can be as simple or as complex as you'd like it to be. And it can open up offshore opportunities for your retirement investment that are unavailable any other way. A self-directed IRA is just like a conventional IRA in all the important ways:

- You can have multiple IRAs, so a self-directed IRA can coexist with others.

- Capital gains, dividends and interest earnings within the account incur no tax liability.

- Contributions are tax deductible (subject to conditions).

- Distributions are taxed as ordinary income and can begin when you turn 59 ½ or if you become disabled.

- You can withdraw funds for qualified unreimbursed medical expenses that are more than 7.5% of your adjusted gross income (AGI), or for qualified higher education expenses for yourself, your children and grandchildren.

- When you die, your spouse can roll both of your IRA accounts into one IRA account.

The big difference is that with a self-directed IRA, a specialist IRA "custodian" permits you actively to choose and design investments far beyond everyday stocks, bonds and mutual funds. You can invest in real estate, private mortgages, private equity, precious metals, intellectual property ... and much else.

You can reap incredible gains, tax-free, both the income from your investments and their underlying appreciation ... gains that go way beyond what a conventional IRA custodian can provide.

And if you like, you can do it outside the U.S.

Who's Who in the IRA Zoo

In strict legal terms, a self-directed IRA is a bit of a misnomer. In most cases — with one important exception that I'll show you — your IRA assets will actually be held by a custodian, like the trustee of a trust. The Internal Revenue Code requires a custodian for all IRAs — and they must be based in the U.S.

The custodian is responsible for records management and safe-keeping of your IRA, processing transactions, filing required IRS reports, issuing statements and other administrative duties on your behalf. Custodial firms generate revenues from fees, not from trading your money for themselves. In fact, your IRA funds must be "segregated" from the firm's own funds, so they're safe if the company goes bust. That's their core business, and they do it for millions of Americans.

But some provide a lot more value for that service than others. There are two types of IRA custodians.

One offers garden-variety securities, such as stocks, bonds and funds. This is what you'll get if you have an IRA with most big U.S. commercial custodians, such as Fidelity, American Express, Entrust or T. Rowe Price. Although you can choose from a variety of investment profiles, most of these plans are focused on the plain-vanilla U.S. market. You can forget about most "alternative" investments ... especially if they are located outside the U.S.

The other type of IRA custodian, often called "self-directed custodian," is willing to entertain alternative investments that you choose yourself. They add value by helping you to decide what your IRA is going to invest in, and if you wish, put them in safe offshore jurisdictions. There aren't many of them, but I watch them carefully to make sure you can access the best of them.

Self-directed IRA custodians allow you, the IRA owner, to choose and design specific investments, or have it done by an independent asset manager (IAM) of your choice, either in the U.S. or abroad. That's the key to supercharging your IRA, DIY-style.

We're at a time when the U.S. economy is looking shaky. Unemployment is down, but there has been a dramatic decrease in labor force participation as well as quality of jobs created. U.S. equities are peaking … at any moment, a U.S. interest-rate hike could bring them crashing down. And the ever-present threat to wealth confiscation looms. That's why these alternative investments are where you want to be.

The World's Your Oyster … Even Oysters Can Be Your Oyster

I've heard of a case of a self-directed IRA investing in an oyster-farming venture … hence the cheeky section title.

But the U.S. Internal Revenue Code places some restrictions on IRA investments, as I will show.

Most mainstream IRA custodians impose additional restrictions of their own, limiting you to garden-variety U.S. investment funds. That's because their job is to generate mass investment in U.S. equity markets, not to allow for customization.

But customization is exactly what you need. That's why self-directed IRA custodians, on the other hand, allow alternative investments, and embrace the increased complexity involved.

What sort of alternative investments are we talking about? The range is enormous … and most of these investments can be in the U.S. or abroad.

In fact, the Internal Revenue Code doesn't describe what a self-directed IRA can invest in, only what it cannot invest in.

Let's start with some of the things people have invested in successfully:

Real estate: A self-directed IRA can purchase any type of real estate, including residential and commercial properties, farmland and raw land — both U.S. and foreign. It can be new construction or renovation of an existing property. Your self-directed IRA funds can be used for purchase, maintenance and expenses such as taxes and utilities. When the property generates income, either from rental or sale, those funds go back to your IRA, tax-free. They can then be used to invest in other assets.

For example, your IRA could buy a home now that you'd plan to use in retirement. Your rental income goes back to your IRA and is used to maintain it, and to fund other investments.

Unlike an annuity or private insurance policy, where you can't self-direct your investments, with a self-directed IRA you can select the property and negotiate the terms of the deal yourself. You just direct your self-directed IRA custodian to pay for the purchase. The custodian must be the legal owner, so all documents associated with the offer and purchase, as well as anything associated with the ownership of the property, must be in the name of the custodian. Although, specifically referencing you as the IRA owner, such as "XXX Company Custodian for Benefit of (Your Name) IRA."

If you wish, real estate purchased in a self-directed IRA can even have a "non-recourse" mortgage against the property (i.e., one where neither you nor the custodian have personal liability for the mortgage — only the property as collateral). That can help leverage your self-directed IRA funds. However, according to Section 514 of the tax code, if you do this on a real estate investment, some of the income from the property will be subject to Unrelated Business Income Tax (UBTI).

Bear in mind that an IRA-owned property won't qualify for tax deductions for property taxes, mortgage interest or depreciation. Also, neither you nor any "disqualified person" may live in or vacation in the property. You can make decisions about how the property is maintained, but you can't do the work yourself. (A disqualified person is basically you and your descendants, as well as any entity that you control. Investments involving your self-directed IRA must always be handled in a way that benefits your retirement account and not you or others close to you right now. Your self-directed IRA has to avoid any investment that would appear to involve immediate benefit for you, any descendants or any entity in which you hold a controlling equity or management interest.)

One of the interesting aspects of real estate in a self-directed IRA is that you could purchase a retirement home for yourself with it. You'd have to avoid any involvement in the property while it is in your IRA, but you could rent it out and use the income to fund renovations and improvements in anticipation of moving in one day. When you do, taking the title of the house will count as a "distribution" from your IRA. You will then pay an ordinary income tax on the appreciation of the house's value since the IRA purchased it, at the current rate.

For example, let's say you establish a self-directed IRA LLC with $100,000 to purchase a house. Assume you operate the LLC open for 10 years and that it appreciates at an average annual rate of 8%. Your rental income is all tax-free, since it all returns to the IRA. After 20 years your $100,000 investment would be worth $215,890, and you'd pay income tax on the $115,890.

Business investments and private equity: Self-directed IRA funds can be invested in private companies. Ownership is usually expressed as a percentage or number of shares of stock. A self-directed IRA can even fund a start-up business or other venture, as long as it's managed by someone other than you or a disqualified person. This is especially attractive if the start-up does well: Your IRA's value will increase along with the fair market value of the company. And of course, it's all tax deferred.

The IRS does put a few restrictions on private equity investments by a self-directed IRA. It can't purchase stocks that you already own. In most cases, neither you nor any disqualified persons can be employed by the company while the IRA has an equity position in that company. Also, the IRA cannot be a general partner in a limited partnership, nor can it invest in an S-Corporation.

Private loans: The IRS also allows self-directed IRAs to make private loans. You can choose the borrower, the principal amount and interest rate, length of the term, payment frequency and amount of the loan, as well as whether or not the loan will be secured. The IRA custodian makes the actual loan in its name, for the benefit of your self-directed IRA. (Such loans cannot be made to yourself, or to prohibited persons.)

Other investments: You can choose self-directed IRA investments based on your own expertise. Depending on your area of specialty, you could direct your self-directed IRA to invest in currencies, commodities, hedge funds, commercial paper, royalty rights, intellectual property or equipment and leases. Self-directed IRAs have invested in golf courses, race horses and mineral rights.

Precious metals: I know that metals are of big interest to people like us. You want them, and you'd prefer them to be offshore. That's smart thinking these days. Fortunately, self-directed IRAs are an ideal way to hold part of your retirement kitty in precious metals.

A self-directed IRA can hold gold, silver, platinum and palladium. The Taxpayer Relief Act of 1997 created this option for you.

The rules for taking distributions from a "gold IRA" are the same as those for a regular IRA. You can liquidate your IRA metals for cash or take physical possession of them. Both actions are equivalent to taking a taxable IRA distribution.

Your self-directed IRA can hold coins — as long as they aren't considered collectibles — and bullion.

- Coins: In order for coins to be held inside a self-directed IRA, they must be 99% pure (or better). They must be "bullion coins," not "collector's coins." That rules out Krugerrands, older Double Eagle gold coins and numismatic coins. Allowed bullion coins include one, one-half, one-quarter or one-tenth ounce U.S. gold coins; other gold coins, such as the Australian Kangaroo/Nugget, Austrian Philharmonic, Canadian Maple Leaf, Australian Kookaburra, Mexican Libertad, Isle of Man Noble and

Australian Koala; one-ounce silver coins minted by the Treasury Department; or any coin issued under the laws of any U.S. state.

- Bullion: Your IRA can hold bullion, such as gold, silver, platinum or palladium in bars, as long as it's of the requisite fineness.

What about storage? Unless you opt to use an LLC as the vehicle for your IRA assets (see below), your bullion coins or bars must be in the physical possession of an IRS-approved trustee, which must be a U.S. bank or approved depository, not a foreign bank. The one exception is the American Gold Eagle coin. Because these are legal tender — like the paper U.S. dollar — they can be held in an offshore account.

Of course, there are other options for including metals in your self-directed IRA:

- The Hard Assets Alliance (HAA), offers you the ability to own gold, stored internationally, inside a pre-existing IRA without having to go through a complex process. That's because they use the American Gold Eagle, which is considered a form of U.S. currency.

- Another IRS-approved option is to buy shares of an exchange-traded fund (ETF) that tracks the value of particular precious metals.

- You can have your self-directed IRA buy stock in a mining company.

LLCs and IRAs: I'm sure you're wondering about the safety of keeping your IRA metals inside the U.S. After all, the federal deficit is about the same amount as the total U.S. retirement savings. That's an ominous thought.

The answer to this threat is an offshore IRA LLC.

In this structure, your self-directed IRA exclusively owns an offshore LLC, and you as the IRA owner become the manager of the LLC. This gives you the ability to manage your retirement funds directly, as long as you play by the "rules."

By forming the LLC offshore, you can hold metals offshore, open brokerage accounts in foreign countries, hold or trade foreign currencies and make more aggressive investments. Plus, you get the added benefit of having your assets securely offshore as an extra layer of protection from the greedy U.S. government.

When you form an offshore IRA LLC, no one has access to or control over your investments but you. Your custodian is merely responsible for moving your IRA assets into your new LLC and for reporting your offshore LLC to the IRS, since it's your only self-directed IRA asset. All the other assets are under the LLC itself.

From there, it's up to you — as a member of the LLC — to determine how and where to invest, including offshore gold or other precious metals.

As an added benefit, the custodian will no longer charge a transaction fee on your investments in the LLC, saving you a lot of money.

When it comes to precious metals offshore, LLCs are critical. Several European banks and other financial institutions are willing to hold American IRAs, offering a variety of precious metal storage programs. But to access them, you must have an offshore LLC — IRS rules prohibit your U.S. custodian from doing this on your behalf.

Sounds too good to be true? Don't worry: It's perfectly legal.

Getting Expert Help

I mentioned that although I'm a DIY guy, I know when to trust the experts. For example, before I start soldering the circuit board on my precious Fender Deluxe Reverb guitar amplifier, I run my plans by a trusted specialist in Seattle who knows a lot more than I do about such matters.

The same applies to your self-directed IRA. Whether your IRA is managed by your custodian or by you via an LLC, you are welcome to use the services of an independent asset manager (IAM) to help you plan and execute your investments. For a fee, the IAM can help you decide what to instruct your custodian to do with your self-directed IRA assets.

This is especially useful — even essential — when it comes to offshore investments, especially via an offshore LLC. IAMs in Europe, for example, have well-developed relationships with European banks and other institutions that can host LLC accounts and arrange precious metal transactions and storage.

And of course they know European markets much better that most U.S. advisers. With the European economy looking up these days, an offshore IAM can help you take advantage of the rising tide.

Play by the Rules

The IRS has rules about IRA investments, and you don't want to break them. They're not too complicated, but it's critical to be aware of them ... especially if you take the offshore LLC route with your self-directed IRA.

Here's why: If the IRS decides that there's been a "prohibited transaction" under Internal Revenue Code Section 4975, your IRA loses its tax exempt status. The entire fair market value of your IRA is treated as a taxable distribution, subject to ordinary income tax. You'd also pay a 15% penalty as well as a 10% early distribution penalty if you're under the age of 59 ½.

You don't want that to happen. But it won't, if you know the rules and obtain and follow good advice from a qualified tax attorney like the ones I recommend.

There are three types of prohibited transactions: those involving specific investments, those involving disqualified persons and self-dealing.

Prohibited investments: Your self-directed IRA can't invest in life insurance. It can't invest in collectibles such as artwork, rugs, antiques, gems, stamps, alcoholic beverages or collectible coins (there are exceptions, as I explained above).

Disqualified persons: This is based on the premise that investments involving your self-directed IRA must always be handled in a way that benefits your retirement account and not you or others close to you right now. Basically, your self-directed IRA has to avoid any investment that would appear to involve immediate benefit for you, any descendants or any entity in which you hold a controlling equity or management interest. That means things such as:

- Borrowing money from your IRA.

- Selling property to your IRA.

- Receiving compensation for managing your IRA.

- Receiving compensation from a disqualified entity, such as a company your IRA owns.

- Personally guaranteeing an IRA loan.

- Using your IRA as security for a personal loan.

- Using it to pay for a personal expense.

- Living in a property owned by your IRA.

Self-dealing and conflict of interest: This is when the IRS can show that you or a disqualified person received some indirect personal benefit from your IRA. Examples include issuing a mortgage on a residence purchased by a disqualified person, or buying stock from yourself, from any entity in which you have a controlling equity position or from a disqualified person.

Fortunately, there are excellent tax attorneys who specialize in staying on top of the rules and case laws involving prohibited transactions … they are an essential part of your self-directed IRA strategy.

How to Convert Your IRA to a Self-Directed IRA

Moving money from your existing IRA (or even from a 401(k) or 403(b)) to a self-directed IRA can be done in two ways. They're both legal and tax-free, as long as they're done the right way.

- A transfer is the method used to move your retirement funds from your existing IRA to a new IRA. In a direct transfer, the distribution check is not sent to you. Instead, your IRA's assets are transferred from your old custodian directly to the custodian of your new self-directed IRA. You can choose to transfer your existing plan at any time, tax-free.

- A rollover is used to move your retirement funds between two qualified retirement plans, such as from your current 401(k) to a self-directed IRA.

With a rollover, the distribution from your existing retirement plan is paid directly to you. This distribution is tax-free as long as you redeposit your funds into your new IRA within 60 days. It is important to note that if the 60-day period is exceeded, you will be liable for taxes and penalties on the funds withdrawn. You may rollover funds from an existing IRA tax-free once per year.

Choosing a Custodian

Self-directed IRA custodians aren't responsible for your investment choices … you are. If you tell them to invest in something that doesn't work out, it's not their problem. Indeed, most IRA agreements clearly state that investors are solely responsible for making investment decisions in connection with their funds.

Some investment promoters seeking self-directed IRA business require exclusive use of certain custodians. With a few exceptions, I'm wary of such arrangements. The exception is when an offshore IAM has an existing relationship with a trusted U.S. custodian and prefers to work with them.

On the other hand, an investment scheme that says "you can buy in as long as you use custodian 'X'" should be treated with caution.

Needless to say, it's critical to choose the right self-directed IRA custodian. Here are some of the things to consider:

Specialization: Make sure you work with an IRA custodian that genuinely specializes in alternative investments. A few IRA custodians will custody both types of investments. An IRA custodian who specializes in traditional investments typically won't be the best choice also to custody your alternative investments.

The reverse holds true as well. When you work with a self-directed IRA custodian, you want one whose specialty matches up with your needs. Remember, you can have more than one IRA.

Fees: Every IRA custodian charges fees for their services. They are often surprisingly low — several hundred dollars to set up and between $100 and $150 a year thereafter. Nevertheless, there are two fee models — either a per-transaction fee model or an asset-based percentage fee model. Make sure the custodian's fee schedule aligns with your investment strategy. Your choice will affect the total returns of your self-directed IRA. The bigger your account, the more negotiating room you'll have when it comes to fees.

Number of transactions: Your investment strategy might involve frequent transactions. Some custodians also offer automated investment services. Make sure your IRA custodian understands and is prepared to handle your investment habits.

Miscellaneous Costs: Many alternative investments provide a variety of services as part of the investment strategy and almost all IRA custodians charge fees for them. They include federal funds wires, notarizing documents, document storage, account setup fees, statement fees, transfer fees, account termination fees and servicing fees such as check writing, processing documents and so on. Some custodians include these services in their custody fees, others itemize the fees and charge them separately. My preference would be for most fees to be included in your custody fees, unless they are unavoidable pass-through fees, such as federal funds wires or postage. Make sure your expected return on investment takes all these miscellaneous fees into account.

Service: This is really the key and why due diligence is so important. You want to consider your custodian's depth of knowledge, timeliness of response, precision, consistency of a process, speed of resolution of any issues and willingness to adapt to a changing environment. Remember, investing in a piece of real estate inside a self-directed IRA requires the custodian to process all documentation associated with the property (e.g., paying taxes, expenses, insurance, maintenance personnel or other expenses). If the service team at the custodian isn't experienced at this, are slow in their response time or are sloppy with their documentation processing, your investments could be negatively affected.

A Final Example

Let's wrap up our tour of self-directed IRAs with an example.

Rob is in his late 50s, self-employed and in the real estate business. He knows U.S. markets reasonably well enough, but he's not convinced that they are the key to his retirement future. He knows property, however, and how to make money out of it.

Rob has three current IRAs: two self-employment IRAs with about $500,000 in each and a Roth IRA with $250,000. He also has an old 401(k) from earlier in his career worth about another $250,000. He wants to keep the Roth as a place to put occasional windfalls. But the two SEP-IRAs are weak performers.

So he decides to look for an appropriate custodian who has a lot of experience in handling U.S. real estate transactions. He also wants to form an offshore Nevis LLC to hold any self-directed IRA property acquisitions, and also so he can open gold accounts in Europe via an independent investment manager.

Rob identifies a suitable custodian and has an attorney to execute due diligence on them. His attorney also advises him on the mechanics of the process of setting up and running his self-directed IRA before he takes the plunge.

When he's ready, he decides to request that his current IRA custodian transfer his two SEP-IRAs to the new self-directed IRA custodian, who invests them in an offshore LLC set up by his attorney. But he decides to take a rollover of his old 401(k), because he wasn't sure whether he wanted to put it into his existing Roth or his new self-directed IRA. New IRS rules, his attorney told him about, stipulate that he can only this once a year — the reason he decided to move his SEP-IRAs by direct custodian-to-custodian transfer.

Within a few months, money that had accumulated in his SEP-IRAs purchased a range of investment properties in the U.S. and abroad that he knew well, thanks to his real estate expertise. He chose high-growth markets in the U.S. and Panama, where returns were in the double-digits. He used about 50% of his IRA value to do that. He put another 30% of his self-directed IRA value into offshore gold storage in Liechtenstein. The remaining 20% he invested in a variety of foreign stocks, bonds and currencies.

With three years, the value of Rob's retirement portfolio had doubled. That's because he had the flexibility to invest in areas he knew intimately.

Before that, he'd just been a spectator as someone else managed his money ... and not very well.

If that sounds like a story you'd like to be part of ... start now. There's no reason to wait.

INCOME SECRET NO. 22:

Use Your "Secret IRA" to Save as Much as $591,000

PLANNING for retirement is no easy task. With the likelihood of Social Security and even pensions failing on the rise with each passing year, the burden of supporting yourself through your golden years is falling more and more on you.

In fact, a GOBankingRates poll revealed that one-third of Americans have no retirement savings and 28.6% have less than $10,000 saved.

But many people are looking for ways to maximize their retirement savings while still getting the best tax benefits. There are, of course, the standard 401(k) and IRA savings plans ... assuming that you are even eligible to enjoy the tax benefits of an IRA.

However, what if you could grow your money for retirement in a "Super IRA" that allows you to invest tax free and withdraw the money without incurring taxes?

I know, it sounds too good to be true.

The truly remarkable thing is that this incredible retirement savings plan isn't technically meant for retirement. It's part of your health insurance.

The health savings account (HSA), or sometimes referred to as an (H)IRA, was created as a way to put more control over health expenses into the hands of individuals in hopes of bringing down costs. When it was pushed through Congress in 2003 as part of the Medicare Prescription Drug, Improvement, and Modernization Act, few realized that it provided Americans with an interest loophole when it came to their retirement savings.

A loophole that could save you as much as $591,000.

What Is an HSA?

A health savings account (HSA) is similar to a regular personal savings account that you stash away for a rainy day. The only difference is that this money is being stored for qualified health care expenses. An HSA can be established with you as the sole beneficiary, or for you plus your spouse and/or dependents.

However, to establish an HSA, you must be enrolled in a high-deductible health plan (HDHP). These HDHPs have much smaller monthly premiums than most health insurance plans, which makes them enticing to individuals who are attempting to cut down on up-front health care costs. The goal of HDHPs is to cover serious injury or illness.

But HDHPs require that you first meet your annual deductible in medical costs each year before your plan starts to pay any benefits. This is where your HSA comes in handy. Out-of-pocket medical expenses that aren't covered by your HDHP can be funded by the savings you've stored away in your HSA.

But what if you don't use all the savings you've stored over the year for medical expenses?

The great thing about the HSA is that it's not a "use it or lose it" scenario. If you don't use all the funds that you've stored in your HSA during the year for medical expenses, then that money rolls over and continues to accumulate.

Year after year. On and on and on … you can see where I'm going with this. It's just like a savings account, but better because the money that you've invested in the HSA is pretax dollars. The savings are growing tax-free. And if you withdraw the money for qualified medical expenses, you won't be taxed on those withdrawn funds either.

That's something an IRA or a 401(k) can't even claim.

The HSA Tax Advantage

The HSA is a great way to save for, as well as pay for, health care expenses, but one of the great added bonuses is that it offers some great tax advantages.

A HSA is largely funded through pretax contributions. For the most part, contributions to your HSA are made through payroll deposits (through your employer) using pretax dollars. Your employer can also make contributions on your behalf, and the contribution is not included in your gross income. As a result, you will owe fewer taxes because your gross annual income is lowered by the amount that you paid into your HSA.

Your Estimated Tax Savings			
Without HSA		**With HSA**	
Gross annual pay (estimate)	$60,000	Gross annual pay (estimate)	$60,000
Estimated tax rate (30%)	-$18,000	Maximum annual family coverage HSA contribution	-$6,750
Net annual pay	=$42,000	Adjusted gross pay	=$53,250
Estimated current + future healthcare expenses	-$6,750	Estimated tax rate (30%)	-$15,975
Final take-home pay	**=$35,250**	Final take-home pay	**=$37,245**
Take home this much more $2,025			

All figures in this table are estimates based on an annual salary of $60,000 and maximum contribution limits to the benefit account. Your salary, tax base, healthcare expenses and tax savings may be different.

What's more, contributions are not subject to state income taxes either (unless you are a resident of Alabama, California or New Jersey — these are the only states that require you to pay state income taxes on your HSA contributions).

But what if you pay into your HSA with after-tax dollars? Don't worry. You're covered. You can deduct any after-tax dollar contributions from your gross income on your tax return.

Now remember that those contributions to the HSA aren't just sitting in cash. That money can be invested in a variety of vehicles such as stocks, bonds, mutual funds and exchange-traded funds. What's more, any growth enjoyed during the year — whether through price appreciation, dividends or interest payments — is also growing free of federal taxes as well as most state taxes. Right now, the only states to tax HSA earnings are New Hampshire and Tennessee.

And finally, with an HSA, withdrawals can be tax-free. Withdrawals from your HSA are not subject to federal (or in most cases, state) income taxes if they are used for qualified medical expenses. As you can see from the table below, other retirement savings plans such as the 401(k), IRA and Roth IRA can't even claim all of those tax benefits.

	401(k)	IRA	Roth IRA	H(IRA)
Tax-free before investing	✓	✓	X	✓
Tax-free while growing	✓	✓	✓	✓
Tax-free withdrawls	X	X	✓	✓

The Other Benefits of an HSA

The tax benefits of an HSA are tempting enough to entice most investors into this kind of savings plan, but those aren't the only advantages offered.

Did you know that other people can actually contribute to your HSA?

Contributions to your health care savings account aren't limited to the funds pulled from your paycheck. In fact, anyone from your employer, your spouse or a relative can add to your HSA. The Kaiser Family Foundation reports that 72% of employers contribute to HSAs — an average $920 for singles and $1,600 for families.

In addition, the funds in your HSA don't disappear at the end of the year if you don't use them. Many people have been burned over the years using flexible spending accounts to help pay for medical expenses.

They would dutifully contribute to the account all year, but if they overestimated what their medical expenses would be and didn't spend all the money ... poof! Gone when the year ended.

That's not the case at all with an HSA. If you have money left in your HSA at the end of the year, it rolls over to the next year. That allows you to keep the money invested and growing for the future and your retirement.

What if you change health insurance plans?

Don't worry. The money is still yours and is available for future qualified medical expenses.

Life comes with many shifts and changes, and you need your HSA to follow you. Should you change your health insurance plans, employer or even retire, your funds will remain in your HSA to grow tax fee.

What if you don't want to bother with mailing in copies of receipts and waiting for reimbursement?

HSAs are far more convenient than other savings accounts as most HSAs issue a debit card. This will allow you to pay for your prescription medication and other expenses right away. If you wait for a bill to come in the mail, you can call the billing center and make a payment over the phone using your debit card. You can even use the card at an ATM to withdraw cash.

The Drawbacks of an HSA

No plan is perfect, and it is critical that you understand the few disadvantages that come with an HSA.

The first and most important is that an HSA requires you to have a high-deductible health plan (HDHP).

And while you may be enjoying smaller insurance premiums each month, it can be difficult — even with help from money in an HSA — to come up with the cash to meet a high deductible.

Furthermore, if you have health care expenses that surpass what you had planned for, you may find that you have not saved enough money in your HSA to cover your costs.

While you can add pretax money, allowing the fund to grow tax free, and even withdraw funds tax free for qualified purchases, there is a chance that you could pay taxes and penalties. If you withdraw funds for nonqualified expenses prior to turning 65, you'll owe taxes on the money withdrawn from the HSA plus a 20% penalty.

After the age of 65, you'll owe only taxes on the money withdrawn, but not the penalty. (Keep in mind that this is a bit different from an IRA, where there's no 10% penalty tax for withdraws from an IRA if you're over the age of 59 ½.)

It is important you are organized, because you will need to keep your receipts to prove that withdrawals from the HSA were used for qualified health expenses.

And finally, some HSAs charge a monthly maintenance fee or a per-transaction fee, which can vary from one institution to another. While these are usually low, they can easily eat away at the savings and growth that you've achieved.

These disadvantages are not insurmountable in the least. They simply require some careful planning, a little bookkeeping, and some research on the best place to set up your HSA to keep fees to a minimum.

Taking Advantage of Qualified Expenses

Health care costs might have finally slowed from their years of double-digit growth, but PwC's Health Research Institute is still predicting a medical-cost increase of 6.5% for 2018, which is substantially higher than our rate of inflation and economic growth in America. What's more, prescription-drug prices are projected to rise 12% throughout the rest of the year.

And even without an HDHP, we find ourselves paying more and more of those medical expenses out of our own pocket — and those expenses tend to skyrocket as we get older.

In fact, Fidelity reports that a 65-year-old couple leaving the workforce today can expect to spend $220,000 on health care.

So why not use tax-free funds to pay for those medical expenses?

The fact is that there are hundreds of health expenses that qualify for tax-free payments from an HSA. Some of those expenses include:

- Acupuncture.
- Alcoholism treatment.
- Ambulance services.
- Chiropractors.

- Contact lens supplies.
- Dental treatments.
- Diagnostic services.
- Doctor's fees.
- Eye exams, glasses and surgery.
- Fertility services.
- Guide dogs.
- Hearing aids and batteries.
- Hospital services.
- Insulin.
- Lab fees.
- Prescription medications.
- Nursing services.
- Surgery.
- Psychiatric care.
- Telephone equipment for the visually or hearing impaired.
- Therapy or counseling.
- Wheelchairs.
- X-rays.

What's more, health insurance premiums are not eligible as qualified medical expenses if you are under the age of 65. However, after the age of 65, you can use the fund from your HSA to pay for health insurance premiums including Medicare Part B premiums and long-term-care insurance premiums.

To see a full list of medical and dental expenses that you can use tax free with your HSA funds, please read the IRS Publication 502, Medical and Dental Expenses (https://www. irs.gov/forms-pubs/about-publication-502).

Can You Open an HSA?

So, you now understand what an HSA is, the advantages and the few disadvantages.

You've gone over your past medical expenses and made estimates on what you think your future medical needs are likely to be.

You believe that an HSA will not only fit your current medical expenses, but that it will allow you to save on taxes that you're paying right now on your income, and grow a nice tax-free nest egg to help fund your retirement.

Yes, it looks like a great plan for you.

But are you eligible?

Just as there are limitations on whether you can deduct your IRA contribution due to your income levels, there are federal guidelines on whether you can open and contribute to an HSA.

To open an HSA, you must be:

- Covered under a HDHP on the first day of the month.
- Not covered by any other non-HDHP plan (with some exceptions for certain plans with limited coverage, such as dental, vision and disability).
- Not enrolled in Medicare.
- Not claimed as a dependent on someone else's tax return.

Each year, the IRS sets up guidelines for HSAs and HDHPs, based on individual and family coverage.

For 2018, all HDHPs must have a minimum deductible of $1,350 for individuals and $2,700 for families. The out-of-pocket maximum (including deductibles, copayments and coinsurance, but not premiums) cannot exceed $6,650 for individuals and $13,300 for families.

As long as you can check all these boxes, you can open an HSA.

Establishing Your HSA

First step, of course, is to join a high-deductible health plan.

Then you can sign up for a health savings account. Your health insurance provider can provide you with more information on setting up an HSA through its recommended bank.

But you don't have to use the bank your health insurance provider recommends … and that might prove to be in your best interest.

Not all HSA providers are equal. Some will require that you hold a minimum amount in cash (which obviously limits the amount that you have invested and growing toward your retirement), and others will have a variety of fees that can cut into your savings.

When you're shopping for the provider of your HSA, here are some things to look for:

- No minimum balance. Most HSAs don't require you to maintain a minimum balance, but some can require that you keep a certain amount in cash to cover potential medical expenses. However, some providers may waive certain fees if you do.

- Beware of fees. Some accounts charge for monthly account maintenance, debit cards and various transactions. Carefully read all information regarding fees and ask questions about any charges that you don't understand.

- Shoot for the highest interest rate. In this environment of low interest rates, finding a good return for your investment isn't an easy task.

  That doesn't mean you can't find some good deals. Some accounts are similar to a regular bank savings account that pays a modest interest rate. Others have an investment option where you can choose securities, such as mutual funds or individual stocks.

- The best payment options. Look for accounts that offer both paper checks and a debit card. This will allow you to pay for medical expenses in just about any situation, either in person or online.

- Get online convenience. Use an account that you can access online for transactions, statements and records. This allows you to save time and makes electronic payments for your medical expenses.

The thing to remember is that unlike medical savings accounts or health reimbursement arrangements that are controlled by employers, an HSA belongs exclusively to you, the account holder. You can spend the funds at your discretion (though nonqualified medical expenses will result in taxes and penalties) and are free to take along with you if you change jobs.

Maximizing Your HSA

Just like with IRAs, there are limits on how much you, your employer or anyone else can contribute to your HSA each year. The IRS makes adjustments to these limits each year based on inflation calculations.

	2017	2018
Individual	$3,400	$3,450
Family	$6,750	$6,900

However, if you are 55 or older, you are permitted to contribute an additional $1,000 as a "catch-up" contribution similar to 401(k) or IRA contributions.

If you are married, and both of you are at the age of 55, each of you can contribute an additional $1,000.

Unfortunately, it gets a little more complicated if you and your spouse aren't both 55 or older. That's because an HSA is in an individual's name — there is no joint HSA even when you have family coverage. Only the person age 55 or older can contribute the additional $1,000 in his or her own name.

If only the husband is 55 or older and the wife contributes $6,750 to her HSA for their family coverage, the husband has to open a separate account for the additional $1,000.

If both husband and wife are age 55 or older, they must have two HSA accounts if they want to contribute the maximum $8,750. There's no way to hit the maximum with only one account.

You can make contributions to your HSA at any time during the calendar year and up to April 15 of the following tax year. Funds can be added to your HSA in regular amounts or in one lump sum.

One great way to fund your HSA is with a one-time tax-free transfer of funds from your IRA to an HSA. This is not like a rollover, as it counts toward your annual HSA contribution limit.

It does allow you to move a small amount of money from an IRA. It's a smart move, particularly if you would have been using those IRA funds to pay medical expenses. In that case, you would have had to pay taxes on that IRA disbursement. If you take the money out of your HSA for medical expenses, you don't have to pay taxes on those funds.

Investing for Tomorrow With Your HSA

One of the key things to remember if you plan to use your HSA as a way to fund your retirement is that you must have funds leftover at the end of the year to roll over into the next year.

While it might seem a little counterintuitive since the HSA was designed to help cover your annual medical costs, the benefits of having a vehicle that allows you to triple the tax benefits can't be overlooked when saving for your retirement.

The more you can have left over at the end of the year from your annual contributions, the better. In fact, many financial planners will argue that to really grow the HSA, you could dedicate it to retirement by paying health costs with other savings. If possible, use other savings to pay for smaller expenses so that you can allow the funds in your HSA to grow.

When you are planning the investments for your HSA, be sure to carefully look over your options and make sure that your HSA custodian will meet your investing needs.

Some custodians offer fewer than 20 mutual funds. While HSA Bank, for example, offers a full brokerage via TD Ameritrade. And HealthSavings Administrators lets you pick from 22 low-cost Vanguard funds.

One way to compare your options is through HSASearch. com.

Keep in mind that your HSA withdrawal strategy can influence your investment strategy. If you are planning to use your HSA to pay for current medical expenses, you may want to avoid substantial stock market investments that can decline at any time and look for liquid investments that conserve principal.

If you are planning to use your HSA more for future medical expenses during your retirement, you may have a longer time frame that will allow you to take on more risk through significant stock investments to grow your nest egg.

In fact, if you can postpone accessing your HSA account until your 80s, when you might have high medical or long-term-care expenses, you would benefit from a very long investing horizon.

When it comes to funding and ranking your retirement accounts, it's important to not only take into account the tax benefits, but the potential penalties on withdrawals as well. It may be best to set your hierarchy of contribution at:

1. 401(k) or IRA up to any match.

2. HSA to contribution limit.

3. 401(k) nonmatched limit.

4. IRA nonmatched limit.

Building Your Retirement With Triple-Tax Benefits

How does the math actually shake out for an HSA over other retirement accounts?

As an example, let's say you start out with $100,000 to invest in your retirement account.

In a Roth IRA, you will have to pay taxes on it at both the state and Federal level. For the sake of simplicity. Let's assume that you pay the U.S. average of 32%, which reduces your initial investment to $68,000.

	401(k)	IRA	Roth IRA	H(IRA)
Tax-free before investing	$100,000	$100,000	$68,000	$100,000
Tax-free while growing	$1,000,000	$1,000,000	$680,000	$1,000,000
Tax-free withdrawls	$680,000	$680,000	$680,000	$1,000,000

As you can see, the HSA is the only account that can truly grow 100% tax free … leaving you with a $1 million retirement. That's an additional $320,000 — money you don't get to keep with an IRA, Roth IRA or 401(k).

Of course, this is a pretty simple example. It assumes you make only one initial deposit and nothing more.

Most people contribute money to their retirement account on a regular basis.

Let's look at another example, where you just put an extra $5,000 into the account each year...

The total amount for each retirement plan would look like this:

	401(k)	IRA	Roth IRA	H(IRA)
Tax-free before investing	$100,000	$100,000	$68,000	$100,000
Tax-free while growing	$1,848,810	$1,848,810	$1,257,191	$1,848,810
Tax-free withdrawls	$1,257,191	$1,257,191	$1,257,191	$1,848,810

As you can see, the 401(k), IRA and Roth IRA end up at nearly the exact same amount … $1,257,191.

But the HSA soars to $1,848,810, thanks to its triple tax benefit — giving you an extra $591,000 for your retirement.

None of those traditional retirement plans can give you this level of freedom.

All you have to do is put your money into an HSA ... and watch it grow.

And, unlike a traditional retirement plan ... you can withdraw money tax free before you are 59 ½ for some of retirement's most worrisome and unexpected expenses ... like health-care costs.

Plus, if you don't need the extra money during retirement, you're not required to take it out. Unlike IRAs, Roth IRAs, and 401(k)s, you can leave it in, and let it grow ... even after you are 70 ½.

The HSA may have been born as out of a health care plan, but it has become the "Super IRA" you need to grow your nest egg and see yourself through a worry-free retirement.

INCOME SECRET NO. 23:

Get Paid $565 a Month, for LIFE, Simply for "Insuring" Your Nest Egg

"Son, you scared the heck out of us."

The two ladies' gentle Southern drawls strained at the burden of speaking of such distasteful matters. Where I live in the Deep South, dignified ladies don't talk to strangers about their financial affairs.

And they hadn't actually said "heck," either. But I wasn't exactly a stranger.

The ladies had been reading *The Bauman Letter* for some time now. They got it as a trial with one of my colleagues' products. If they weren't sure about renewing before, they certainly were now, they told me.

We had just emerged from one of my presentations at the recent Total Wealth Symposium in Hollywood, Florida. I'd spoken about something I call the "red zone" — the five years before and after retirement.

It's the decade of your life that matters most … at least when it comes to the way you'll be able to live the rest of it.

I had just presented a chart showing what happens when you retire in a down market and have to liquidate stocks at discount prices to satisfy the IRS' required minimum distribution (RMD) requirements — or simply to survive.

Not to mention supporting an Oscar de la Renta shopping habit.

Taking distributions from a stock portfolio during a historically average 34%, 18-month long bear market drop would mean running out of money in 20 years instead of 30, I'd warned.

I showed scarier charts illustrating why I feel the current bull market is at its top. Lots of red.

"Low interest rates have lashed investors into a stampede to equities that has little to do with the underlying economy or future earnings," I'd said. Everyone is chasing yield ... often using dangerous margin debt to leverage their investments. It's like a loaded mousetrap.

Testing the convention against mixed metaphors, I'd gone on to compare markets to a ballistic missile. A rocket keeps going upward for a while even after the motor cuts out. But gravity ensures that it starts to curve downward at an ever-accelerating pace.

Thus terrified, the ladies had asked to know more about my *Alpha Stock Alert* service, designed to hedge such calamities before they happen.

"But there is another way to avoid running out of money, as well," I told them. Their blue eyes stared at me as if I were the Delphic oracle itself. At least I knew I was making more sense that a half-drugged chief priestess of Apollo.

"But it requires adopting an attitude like Zen Buddhism. You have to take a leap of faith. You need equanimity." I wasn't sure how well references to the Buddha played in Baptist country, but it seemed OK. And I was deep in mixed-metaphor territory now.

"I don't mean pure faith without evidence. In fact, as the Dalai Lama himself would tell you, true faith is always backed by empirical science. I simply mean having faith that what you are doing is the wisest course based on all the factors at play and all the information available ... even if others are telling you differently based on less rational forms of faith."

This Income Secret is about the money-preserving strategy I offered the ladies: The humble annuity.

After all, it's the only thing guaranteed to ensure that you don't run out of money in retirement.

After all, that's the single most common concern I hear from my faithful readers of *The Bauman Letter*.

Why an Annuity?

Let's get one thing straight: If you haven't retired yet, you shouldn't consider investing in an annuity unless you are already contributing the maximum to other retirement plans, such as an individual retirement account (IRA) or 401(k).

That's because traditional retirement plans provide the same tax deferral as annuities — but without the fees (more on that in a moment). Of course, you can invest in an annuity inside a tax-advantaged account, as I've suggested in previous *Bauman Letter* reports, but you get no extra tax benefit.

Also, be aware that early-withdrawal penalties and surrender (early termination) fees mean an annuity is useless for short-term saving. You'd need to hold a variable annuity at least 15 years for the benefits of tax deferral to outweigh the extra costs.

That means the ideal pre-retirement annuity buyer is someone:

- Who is making the maximum contributions to other retirement plans.

- Who can live without the money until after age 59 1/2.

- Who is in at least the 25% tax bracket to take advantage of the tax deferral.

But that's only relevant to folks still working. The focus here is on those in the "red zone" — five years before and five years after retirement (or longer). If that's you, you also might be a viable candidate if you're concerned about outliving your savings … as so many of my readers are.

That's because annuities can provide a guaranteed stream of income in retirement. Here are some pros:

1. To provide a hedge against longer life spans.

According to the Centers for Disease Control, people who were 65 years old in 2017 will likely live into their 80s. After reaching 65, men can expect to live another 18 years and women an additional 20.5 years.

The longer you expect to live, the more annuities make sense. A longer life span means your money needs to last longer, too.

Because annuities provide a guaranteed lifetime income, you can avoid depleting all your assets. And since an annuity is a form of insurance, some of the "longevity risk" — the risk of running out of money — moves to the company offering the annuity product.

2. To impose budget discipline.

Annuities help — no, force — you to manage your money better. Because the payouts are predetermined and the form of annuity I'm going to recommend can't be cashed in, you must live within your means.

As many retirees know, it's easy to tap your retirement portfolio more often than you intend. The biggest threat is "lifestyle creep." You start retirement with 75% of your expenses covered by a pension or other stable monthly income source, but five years later, it's down to 50%. It's all those extra trips to see the grandkids or vacations in Saint Maarten.

The bottom line is that with the right annuity, you can spend only what it's going to pay out every month.

Of course, you can generate additional income beyond your annuity payments, but the annuity becomes your baseline.

3. To ensure peace of mind.

You may be a risk-taker. I know I am. But retirement has a funny way of curing you of that ... and fast.

I hear from many folks who are essentially forced to gamble on high-risk investments because they don't have enough money to last. They take huge risks ... and, as is often the case, they lose.

On the other hand, many people are forced to sell stocks during a big market pullback — or worse, they panic. Selling a large chunk of your portfolio in a down market means you'll have less equity to generate income over the rest of your retirement.

Consider two 30-year periods. The first has three down years, minus 20%, minus 15% and minus 10%, followed by an average annualized return of 6% over 30 years. The second 30-year period has exactly the reverse sequence of returns — average annualized returns of 6% over 30 years with three down years at the very end.

With a $500,000 portfolio with an initial 5% annual withdrawal, the first model runs out of money in 20 years. The second never does.

By forcibly preserving capital in the present and generating guaranteed income in the future, the right annuity can ensure that you don't end up like the first model.

How Do Annuities Work?

Oddly, annuities are insurance products, even though we tend to think of them in terms of investment.

To start one, you make a payment to an insurer — either an up-front lump sum or a series of payments over time. The money grows tax-deferred, like a traditional IRA or 401(k), at a fixed or variable rate — the "accumulation phase."

You pay taxes at regular income rates when you take annuity payments, which the insurer undertakes to make to you for the rest of your life — the "payout phase."

The thing that makes an annuity an insurance product is the guaranteed payouts. Even if the insurer loses money on its investments, it is still obligated to pay you. Moreover, annuities can also include a death benefit. This entitles the beneficiary of the annuity — a spouse or children — to the value of your annuity or a guaranteed minimum, whichever is greater.

There are two types of annuities: deferred and immediate. The distinction overlaps with the "accumulation" and "payout" phases of annuities. Here's why.

Accumulation Phase Annuities: Deferred

There are three subtypes of accumulation annuities: fixed deferred, indexed and variable. The key variable is how much exposure to the equity market they involve.

With a fixed deferred annuity, you lock in a guaranteed rate of return for periods ranging from one year to 10 years. They offer a guaranteed interest rate for a certain term, such as five or 10 years. The rate is set by the insurer, based on market rates. It can fluctuate, but will never drop below your guaranteed rate.

As a result, you won't lose money, but you won't have the potential for growth you'd get by investing in stocks or stock funds. A fixed-rate annuity is worth considering if you have low risk tolerance and a shorter time horizon to retirement.

Fixed deferred annuities are like certificates of deposit (CD). As with a CD, if you hold the money in the annuity to maturity, you will receive a scheduled amount of interest. Unlike a CD, the annuity's interest isn't taxed along the way. Tax is deferred until the earnings are withdrawn.

If you pull your money out before the term ends, however, you could incur a surrender charge. At the end of the annuity's term, the insurer will offer a renewal rate with no new surrender charges.

Indexed annuities are a type of fixed deferred annuity with a growth rate pegged to the performance of an equity index over a certain term, such as the S&P 500. But the money isn't invested directly into the market. Instead, the market becomes the benchmark for your interest payout.

The key with these annuities is understanding the formula behind your return. You might have a "participation rate" of 50% of S&P 500 Index gains during the contract term. If the market rises 10%, you're only going to get 5%. If the market falls, it has a floor, which is generally zero.

While some indexed annuities are tied to the performance of a well-known index, others are tied to one developed by the insurance company. Make sure you ask what investments comprise the index.

The surrender period is usually seven or 10 years for indexed annuities.

A variable annuity is the riskiest type. Your money is invested in accounts that are like mutual funds.

You can see substantial gains — or the opposite. That means you have unlimited upside but also unlimited downside. It is possible, however, to buy some downside protection by paying extra for a rider that offers a guaranteed minimum withdrawal benefit.

You defer paying tax on earnings while your money is invested by the annuity. You can take a cash distribution after the annuity reaches maturity, and without IRS penalties, after age 59 ½. Those withdrawals are taxable at your ordinary income rate. Because you contributed post-tax money to the annuity, however, part of the payout will be considered a return of capital and not taxable.

When a variable annuity matures, you can choose to "annuitize" it: You turn the accumulated money into an immediate annuity, which I will discuss below.

Payout Phase Annuities: Immediate

There is nothing preventing you from buying deferred annuities in retirement. But because the surrender period is typically seven to 10 years — and life is uncertain — many people avoid deferred annuities, which are inaccessible until maturity, in favor of immediate annuities.

With immediate annuities, you turn over a lump sum to the insurer, who agrees to give you guaranteed payouts over a certain term — 10 to 20 years, perhaps — or for as long as you live. The guarantees never change. Payouts begin anytime within 13 months of starting the annuity.

The most important variables with an immediate annuity are the size of the contract and the interest rate. But age is important too. The older you are when you buy, the bigger your regular payouts.

That's because immediate annuities are based on actuarial values of life span. The insurance company looks at your age and possibly your health and lifestyle, and estimates how long you are expected to live. It then designs the payout of the annuity based on that lifespan.

That means men and women receive different payouts for the same size of annuity and interest rate. Women have longer average lifespans, so their payouts are smaller than men's.

Immediate annuities also offer the flexibility of inflation adjustments and death benefits. For example, you could buy a rider that provides five years of income to you or your beneficiaries, or lets you or your heirs receive your full investment. But there's a cost: Reducing risk this way reduces the payout.

For example, a 72-year-old man in Washington, D.C., who invests $100,000 will receive about $675 in immediate lifetime monthly income. But that payout would be cut to $579 a month if he opted for an heir to receive a lump sum of any premium balance at his death.

Interest Rates and "Laddering"

In recent years, low interest rates have depressed monthly annuity payments. But rates have begun to move up and are expected to climb higher. As a result, annuity payouts are rising as well.

For example, right now, a 65-year-old Georgia man who invests $100,000 in a single-life immediate annuity would receive an average monthly payment of $543. The average monthly payment was $506 in late 2016. That's a 7.3% difference in less than a year.

But there's a risk in waiting for interest rates to rise to buy an immediate annuity.

The Federal Reserve has signaled that it plans more hikes. That may prompt you to postpone an annuity purchase until those hikes take effect. But if the market nose-dives, the Fed could put off those increases or reverse them. Buying an annuity then would mean you take a chance to lock in current rates.

One way around this problem is to build an annuity ladder.

Say you have $300,000 to invest in an immediate annuity. You would invest $100,000 this year, another $100,000 in two years and the remaining $100,000 the year after that. By spreading out your purchases, you'd potentially benefit from higher interest rates in later years.

Laddering also allows you to vary the type of annuity. Immediate annuities can be tailored to all sorts of variables. You can specify the number of years you get guaranteed income. You can include life insurance. You can opt for an immediate payout rider.

Here's a table showing the options available to a 65-year-old man in Georgia, where I live:

Life	$543
Life insurance & 5 years guaranteed	$542
Life insurance & 10 years guaranteed	$532
Life insurance & 15 years guaranteed	$514
Life insurance & 20 years guaranteed	$489
Life insurance with cash refund	$492
5-year period guaranteed	$1,705
10-year period guaranteed	$914
15-year period guaranteed	$661
20-year period guaranteed	$546
25-year period guaranteed	$482

As you can see, you have many options — each of which can be implemented for each annuity in your ladder.

How Much?

Even if I've convinced you to consider an annuity, don't put your entire portfolio into one. That's certainly not what I'm suggesting!

Instead, add up your guaranteed income sources, including Social Security. Then add up your basic expenses, such as housing costs and food. Don't cheat. Factor in nonessential things you know you'll be doing, like traveling and buying gifts for the grandkids.

If there's a gap between your steady income and these essential expenses, buy an immediate annuity to fill it and no more.

That allows you to use the rest of your retirement funds to play the market — to the extent of your risk preferences, of course.

To take an admittedly self-interested example, if you set up your laddered annuity plan and then invested $100,000 in my *Smart Money* system, your pretax return at the end of August would look like this compared to the S&P 500:

Investment: $100,000	
Smart Money return	$10,569.45
S&P 500 return	$4,886.64
Excess: $5,682.80 • Excess %: 116%	

That extra return is a nice trip to the Bahamas, or a lot of presents at Christmas.

Of course, the *Smart Money* system is quite low- risk, so it might be possible to do even better if you have the appetite for it.

Beware of the Fees Monster

A recent study by Senator Elizabeth Warren (D-Mass.) examined 15 major annuity providers. It found that all but two offer perks to reward agents for selling their products. The perks include cruises, luxury car leases, theater tickets and golf outings. None of the companies clearly disclosed the sales incentives to annuity purchasers.

Sales rewards like these drive advisers to recommend an annuity based on his reward, not your needs. Here's how to combat that.

First, when you shop for an annuity, ask two questions, and don't let the salesperson distract you from them:

- What do you want the annuity to guarantee?

- When do you want that guarantee to start?

Second, avoid being distracted by "hypothetical return" illustrations or costly bells and whistles, such as stepped-up death benefits, that you may not really need. Focus on the bottom line.

Third, ask the agent to show you annuities from multiple companies. If he's only offering products from a single company, or if you're having trouble comparing different products, seek out another opinion from another agent, and pit them against each other.

Third, as you narrow your options, ask for a "specimen policy." This is a copy of the actual contract you'd receive after purchasing the annuity. It will help ensure that you see everything before buying.

Finally, after purchasing an annuity, you typically have a "free look" period of about 10 to 30 days, depending on your state. You can review all the details of the contract … and if you decide you've made a mistake, you can terminate it and get a full refund.

Don't Choose Poorly

In the great flick "Indiana Jones and the Last Crusade," there's a memorable scene where a greedy Nazi drinks from the wrong cup and disintegrates into dust. The ancient knight who's been guarding the real grail comments drily: "He chose poorly."

That sense of caution applies to annuities, too, although the stakes aren't so high — and the odds are far, far better than picking one cup out of dozens. That's because in addition to interest rates and actuarial values, immediate annuities can vary based on the financial strength of the insurer.

There are two issues involved: your return and the safety of your money.

First, all else being equal, an insurer with a high credit rating will be able to finance their operations at lower rates. That means they will be able to pay higher average payouts than other insurers.

Second, the insurer's rating also offers the expectation of financial stability. If you're using annuities to generate income over two or three decades, you want to make sure the insurer will be around for the whole time.

That raises an issue that many people ask me: What happens if an insurer goes bankrupt, like a bad holy grail copy?

Unlike bank accounts and other types of financial accounts, annuities are governed by state law, not federal law. Each state has its own rules and regulations, and the degree to which they ensure annuities depends a lot on the size of the state's insurance guaranty association pool. That's one reason why many annuity insurers are clustered in states like New York, which have large insurance pools.

The good news is that only six insurers licensed to sell annuities and life insurance have entered receivership since 2008, and most were small, regional companies. Even so, protect your investment by narrowing your search to insurers rated A-minus or better.

Above all, find out how much of your investment is covered by the state's insurance guaranty association. Most state guaranty associations cover $250,000 or more in annuity benefits per insurer. (You can check state guaranty limits at the National Organization of Life & Health Insurance Guaranty Associations, at www.nolhga.com.) If you plan to invest more than your state's limit, divide your money among several companies.

Conclusion

Annuities are a great option if you are uncertain about how long your money can last. As long as you discipline yourself and are realistic about your expenses over the years to come, you can decide how much to put into this type of product — which is essentially "income insurance."

But be careful. As one commenter has said, annuities are the "Wild West" of U.S. financial markets. Salesmen have powerful incentives to sell you products that may not be your best choice.

So, shop for an annuity the way you'd shop for something in which you take a special interest. For me, it's guitars. For you, perhaps it's cars or jewelry.

In other words, don't buy the first thing that comes along. Look for the absolute best you can get for your money.

After all, it's a big chunk of all the money you're ever going to have.

INCOME SECRET NO. 24:

13 States That Won't Loot Your Retirement

I met Billy at the county dump.

"Salt of the earth." Billy was it.

If there was a uniform for his part of the country, Billy was wearing it. Black work boots, heavy dark-blue cotton work pants, a lighter-blue short-sleeved shirt with his name on it, and a baseball cap with mesh on the back and sides for ventilation in the Virginia heat.

He had a face like a gnarled oak tree … one sunburned by years of working as a Chesapeake Bay waterman. By the looks of it, he'd been chewing tobacco while he was at it.

Billy was born in a house near the village where I was staying.

He was still living in the same house. But the taxes were getting high, he complained.

Didn't he already own his family plot? Why did he have to keep paying for it?

Billy got me thinking.

If you graphed the proportion of Americans who lived their entire lives in a small radius around their birthplace, over time, what would the curve look like?

It was flat from the birth of the United States until the Civil War. After that, the upheavals of Reconstruction sent it downward. It maintained a steady fall until the Depression, when the pace picked up, driven by refugees from the Dust Bowl and jobless migrants in search of work.

The decline began to gather steam after World War II. Industrialization, the GI Bill, the automobile and openness to the outside world got many Americans moving. The pace quickened again in the 1980s, when the deindustrialization of America's manufacturing heartland sent the jobless packing.

But even now, more than a third of Americans live in the same town where they were born and raised. Another 20% live in the same state.

There's a lot of regional variation. About half of Midwesterners live near where they were born. Only a third of Western state residents do. Three-quarters of people in the big cities must call long distance to talk to mom and dad.

But here's the funny thing. In the last 30 years or so, that trend has slowed and started to reverse.

Americans have become less mobile than they were in the second half of the 20th century. More two-job households, an illiquid rural housing market and the high cost of city living have kept people from moving around.

But there's other factors ... the weakness of the U.S. social safety net and our chronic lack of retirement savings.

Stuck in a Retirement Rut

Families without alternative child care need to live near parents and grandparents to look after the little ones while they work. Families with an unemployed breadwinner need to rely on relatives for support until they get back on their feet.

And elders with only Social Security to go on depend on their kids to help.

But that immobility doesn't always make sense ... after all, some parts of the United States are a lot more expensive than others.

At what point does it make more sense to move somewhere less expensive when you retire? After all, the gap between the highest cost of living states and the lowest is so big that retirees who live in the latter have enough extra money to travel home to see the kids and grandkids several times a year.

I don't think that calculation had anything to do with why Billy was still living in Tidewater, Virginia. It was all he'd ever needed. No point in change just for the sake of it.

But it came with a cost for Billy. Virginia levies income taxes and sales taxes. He lived in a county that levies property taxes. Since he lives near the water, the plot of earth where he was born and lived was worth a lot. Health care costs are higher there than in half of U.S. states.

What about you? Have you ever run the numbers to see whether it would make sense to migrate somewhere less expensive in retirement?

If not, this book is your chance to start. I've taken a hard look at the pros and cons of retiring in various parts of these United States. I looked at taxes, the cost of health care and the cost of living.

Money isn't everything, of course. Family ties and geography also matter.

But with a nearly bankrupt government, a refusal to fund the Social Security system, diminishing returns in the stock market and the extinction of private pensions, money matters a lot more than it used to.

That means the choice of your home in retirement does, too.

Households run by someone 65 or older spend an average of $45,756 a year, or roughly $3,800 a month.

How much will you spend? How much can *you* afford?

The Things That Matter

Most people don't think much about the question: "Why do we live where we do?" It's a given.

Maybe, like Billy, you've lived in one place your whole life. Or, like me, you've lived in various places and have settled down in one because it's convenient.

That's not to say that people don't have dreams about living somewhere else. Many people would like to live somewhere abroad perfectly suited to their wants and needs. The obstacle to realizing this dream is often financial. Besides the expense of living in a beautiful foreign environment, there are often high financial requirements for retirement visas.

On the other hand, thousands of Americans have moved abroad because the cost of living is cheaper than the U.S. For example, most people don't think of Ecuador when it comes to retirement in Latin America — but it's one of the most popular destinations, thanks to its easy lifestyle and low cost of living.

But the same logic applies within the United States. Consider the following examples:

- Paul and Alecia have always loved Cape Cod. It would be their perfect retirement location. But property on the Cape is expensive. As much as the environment would suit their lifestyle, acquiring a home there would dig far too deeply into their retirement kitty. And Massachusetts income and property taxes would eat up a lot of their monthly income.

- Stephen and Rita, on the other hand, love the mountains. But they wanted to make their retirement stretch as far as possible, so they decided to pull up stakes and move to Idaho. Property is cheap, and the cost of living is among the lowest in the U.S. The downside is that health care and health insurance are more expensive in the rural part of the state where they live.

- Dan and Emma have lived their whole lives in upstate New York. They'd like to move somewhere warmer and closer to their children and grandchildren. But the high taxes and high cost of living in the state have cut into their income over the years, reducing the amount they've been able to save for their retirement. At least their house is paid for. They've convinced themselves that they're stuck. But those New York state income and property taxes aren't going down anytime soon. In fact, things are getting worse thanks to the recent tax overhaul, which limited their deductibility. On top of that, health care in New York is the most expensive in the country.

One thing jumps out from all these examples: There are many variables to consider. Maintaining the same standard of living in various parts of the country can require radically different incomes.

That means, besides things like crime, culture, weather, amenities, attractions and senior citizen well-being, you need to consider the "brass tacks," as well:

- What's the overall cost of living?

- What is the state tax burden?

- How much does the state tax structure matter, given your specific retirement strategy?

- What's the cost of housing?

- How much will health care cost you?

As you can see, this all involves trade-offs. Clearly, we need a framework!

Values and Cents

Having a firm grasp of your likes and dislikes is the first step to creating a framework to identify the perfect place to retire inside the U.S. Knowing beforehand the things you'll get — and the things you'll lose — when you move to a new state is critical. And you'll never know which of those things are truly the most important to you until you sit down and think about it honestly.

However, I'm going to focus on the financial variables. I'm going to take it as a given that you know your own preferences when it comes to things like weather, culture, city versus country life, and so on. Because, ultimately, it all depends on whether you can afford to live your dream retirement.

Nevertheless, I encourage you to keep your lifestyle values in the back of your mind. As I was researching for this income secret, I came across some data that showed that six of the least-expensive states to live in were also in a list of the 10 worst states for retirement!

In other words, it's not all about money. Some very inexpensive locales are also unpleasant places to live.

Let's start our assessment with the most important variable of all.

Cost of Living

Surveys of retirees routinely show that cost of living is the most important issue determining retirement strategies.

As I researched, I came across many different tabulations of state-by-state cost of living. Ranking states this way is harder than it looks. One reason is that nonfinancial factors can affect the cost of living.

For example, the high cost of living in a place like Vermont or Maryland can be offset by the many free or low-cost things to do, such as skiing in Vermont or boating on the Chesapeake Bay.

The reverse is also true. You could move to a low-cost state like Arkansas or Alabama and be bored to death ... forcing you to spend lots of money traveling elsewhere.

Another complication is that cost of living is tangled up with taxation and the cost of health care, two of our other critical variables. The best rankings of cost of living take this into account.

Eventually I decided to use an index that included costs associated with six categories: housing, utilities, groceries, health care, transportation and miscellaneous expenses. Taxation is excluded.

On the next page are the 10 cheapest and 10 most expensive states on that list.

As I said earlier, there is a clear pattern. The cheaper states are clustered in the Deep South and the lower Midwest. The most expensive states are in the Northeast or on the Pacific. (My own home state, Maryland, is a bit of an outlier ... the inflated cost of living in the D.C. suburbs skews the state, even though many parts of it are more affordable.)

The next five lowest-cost states are Texas, Nebraska, Georgia (my current home), Iowa and Wyoming. Rounding out the top 20 are Utah, Ohio, Michigan and North Carolina.

That gives you a lot of options geographically and climatically.

10 Cheapest Cost of Living States		10 Most Expensive Cost of Living States	
1	Mississippi	1	Hawaii
2	Arkansas	2	California
3	Oklahoma	3	Alaska
4	Indiana	4	Connecticut
5	Idaho	5	New York
6	Tennessee	6	Massachusetts
7	Alabama	7	Maryland
8	Kansas	8	Vermont
9	Missouri	9	Rhode Island
10	Kentucky	10	New Jersey

Taxation

Determining a state's tax burden is also complicated. In addition to income tax, you must also consider property and sales taxes. Another important consideration is whether the state taxes Social Security benefits, and how it treats retirement investment income.

The table on the next page lists the 10 highest and 10 lowest tax states.

The highest tax states have several features in common. They tend to be in the Northeast, which is highly urbanized, densely populated and has a lot of transportation infrastructure to maintain. They tend to be "blue" states politically and make significant investments in social services for their residents. (That accounts for the presence of Minnesota and California in the mix.)

Hawaii's high tax burden is a result of its unique location, its strong social services system, and, above all, high property values and, thus, property taxes.

Top 10 States With the Highest Taxes		Top 10 States With the Lowest Taxes	
1	New York	1	Alaska
2	Hawaii	2	Delaware
3	Maine	3	Tennessee
4	Vermont	4	Florida*
5	Minnesota	5	New Hampshire
6	Connecticut	6	Oklahoma
7	Rhode Island	7	South Dakota*
8	Illinois	8	Alabama
9	New Jersey	9	Montana
10	California	10	Virginia
			* No income tax

On the other hand, four of the 10 lowest tax states have no income tax. The other six states have an income tax, but it's either so low or so favorable to retirees that they are still considered comparatively low tax.

There are, in fact, eight U.S. states that levy no income tax: Nevada, Texas, Washington, Wyoming, South Dakota, Florida, Tennessee and Alaska. (Once you've established residency in Alaska, the state actually pays you every year from its oil industry trust fund.)

But again, as I mentioned above, much depends on how you plan to finance your retirement. All else being equal, if you were going to continue receiving business income in retirement — say you continue to retain ownership interest in a medical practice, or a car dealership or some other family business — you'd want to live in a state with low or no income tax, especially on out-of-state income.

On the other hand, if you were going to rely largely on Social Security benefits, the income tax system wouldn't matter as much as whether those benefits were subject to taxation. In fact, 36 U.S. states don't tax Social Security benefits. Eight of them have no income tax at all, and one — Alaska — has no sales tax:

States With No Social Security Tax		
Alabama	Iowa	Ohio
Alaska*	Kentucky	Oklahoma
Arizona	Louisiana	Oregon
Arkansas	Maine	Pennsylvania
California	Maryland	South Carolina
Delaware	Massachusetts	South Dakota*
Florida*	Mississippi	Tennessee*
Georgia	Nevada*	Texas*
Hawaii	New Hampshire	Virginia
Idaho	New Jersey	Washington*
Illinois	New York	West Virginia
Indiana	North Carolina	Wyoming*
		* No income tax

If you look for overlaps in the two tables, you'll find 10 states that are at the bottom of the tax burden list that also don't tax Social Security benefits. They are Wyoming, South Carolina, Idaho, Virginia, Alabama, South Dakota, Oklahoma, New Hampshire, Florida, Tennessee, Delaware and Alaska.

Of those 10, Idaho, Alabama, Oklahoma, and Tennessee are all amongst the 10 lowest cost of living states in the country. Rounding out the top 20 are Georgia, Texas, Wyoming and Ohio.

One of the biggest components of America's cost of living is housing. For a variety of reasons, the cost of a place to "be" in the United States has skyrocketed over the last two generations.

Of course, as with everything else, this rise has been uneven. The fastest rise in housing costs has been in the older cities of the Northeast, coastal Florida, the urban areas of Texas and practically everywhere west of the Great Plains.

By contrast, housing prices have not risen much in the last 20 years in the Midwestern states around the Great Lakes, or in the small towns and rural areas of the South and the Plains states.

Overall, the states with the most affordable housing costs are geographically within the same range as lowest cost of living states. They are located between the Appalachians in the east and the Great Plains in the west, and between the inland regions of the Deep South and the Great Lakes and Canadian border.

That doesn't tell the whole story, however. After housing, the second biggest expenditure for retirees is transportation. For most people that means a car or two, fuel, maintenance and insurance.

Housing

One of the defining features of the states with a low-cost housing environment is lack of good public transportation systems. Few of the cities in the big swath of Middle America where housing is cheap have well-developed train systems. That means a car is a necessity.

Housing Affordability Rank			
1	Ohio	11	Missouri
2	Iowa	12	Kentucky
3	Indiana	13	Wisconsin
4	Nebraska	14	North Dakota
5	Michigan	15	Minnesota
6	Oklahoma	16	Illinois
7	Kansas	17	Arkansas
8	West Virginia	18	Georgia
9	South Dakota	19	Connecticut
10	Pennsylvania	20	Louisiana

On the other hand, popular retirement states like Florida also have poor public transport, but their low tax burdens offset this to a degree.

Once again, this highlights the importance of trade-offs in determining the best environment for retirement … and therefore of doing your homework to see the best fit for you.

The Big Picture

A widely accepted rule of thumb is that you'll need to replace from 70% to 90% of your preretirement income to maintain your standard of living in retirement.

That suggests that the first step to discovering the best value in retirement locales is to compare where you are now — like Billy — with where you might go. The two calculators at the links on the next page allow you to do just that. They show you how far your expected retirement income will go in different locales:

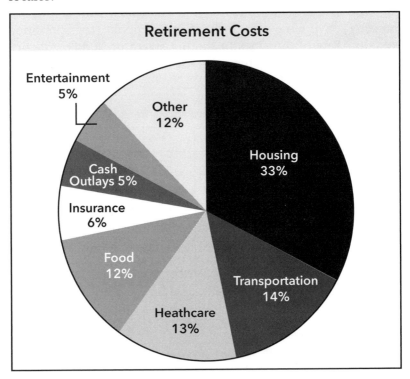

- https://smartasset.com/mortgage/cost-of-living-calculator

- https://money.cnn.com/calculator/pf/cost-of-living/index.html

For example, the first calculator shows that you'd need to have an income of $50,279 in El Paso, Texas, to have the same standard of living that $65,000 provides in Boston — a drop of 23%!

The second calculator shows that you'd save 62% on housing, 38% on utilities and 28% on health care by moving to the city on the banks of the Rio Grande.

Finally, using these techniques, I came up with my own list of the 30 cheapest cities to retire in the U.S. The cheapest is indeed El Paso ... indeed, seven of the 10 cheapest places to retire in the U.S. are in the Lone Star State.

30 Cheapest Cities for Retirement			
1	El Paso, TX	16	Greensboro, NC
2	Brownsville, TX	17	Mobile, AL
3	Fort Wayne, IN	18	Louisville, KY
4	Pasadena, TX	19	Beaumont, TX
5	Amarillo, TX	20	Fayetteville, NC
6	Corpus Christi, TX	21	Tulsa, OK
7	Laredo, TX	22	Columbus, OH
8	Montgomery, AL	23	Akron, OH
9	Lexington, KY	24	Birmingham, AL
10	Lubbock, TX	25	Augusta, GA
11	Oklahoma City, OK	26	Des Moines, IA
12	Columbus, GA	27	Macon, GA
13	Omaha, NE	28	Wichita, KS
14	Winston-Salem, NC	29	Huntsville, AL
15	Pittsburgh, PA	30	Shreveport, LA

Unfortunately for Billy, none of these low-cost locales are in Tidewater, Virginia. Whether he — or you — would benefit by making a move in retirement is all down to the numbers.

Unlike Billy, though, you've got this book to give you a head start.

TRAVEL

Jumping on a plane and flying off to some remote spot in the country or even around the world has long represented a chance for adventure, exploration, and even relaxation — as well as a big drain on your wallet. But you can easily turn your vacation into a source of steady income. In this section, learn about the island escape that's far cheaper than you might expect for this exotic location, how to make money living in amazing homes, and even how you can live in your dream location and get paid for it. Get paid to take that next vacation.

INCOME SECRET NO. 25:

That's the Spirit: Use This "Gift-Giving" Key to a Bon Voyage

What could be better than a fun-filled, relaxing sea cruise?

How about a fun-filled, relaxing sea cruise where the drinks are about one-third the usual cost?

Too good to be true? Not if you're traveling on a cruise line that allows you to purchase a "bon voyage" gift for yourself in the form of pre-cruise orders of wine, beer or liquor.

Instead of paying individually for drinks or running up a huge bar tab during your cruise, you can purchase an alcohol-inclusive drinks package before you depart. These preordered beverages can be two to three times cheaper than individual drinks, and they'll even deliver them to your cabin before the cruise embarks. Whether you prefer top-shelf cocktails or vintage wines, with this nifty travel tip you can sip like royalty all cruise long for a fraction of the cost.

Most mainstream cruise lines allow passengers to pay one base price that covers most — if not all — nonalcoholic and alcoholic drinks onboard. It's a great way to save money and reduce the overall cost of the cruise.

There are a variety of standard, premium, elite and ultimate packages ranging in price from as little as $14.50 to $63.19 per person, per day. Depending on how many members are in your travel party and how much you imbibe, it can save you hundreds of dollars per cruise.

Besides the cost savings, preordering drinks has other advantages:

- **It's easy and convenient.** Beverage packages make the process of ordering drinks as simple as placing your order, having your card swiped and getting whatever you order.

- **There's plenty of selection.** There are multiple levels of cruise beverage packages ranging from soda only to basic packages that also include bottled waters, beers, wines, coffee and cocktails to premium plans that include fine wines, liquors and liqueurs. So, if you're a teetotaler, you can still enjoy a wide selection of nonalcoholic beverages at a much more reasonable price.

- **You can sample as you like.** Beverage packages enable you to try drinks you've never had before. And if you don't like one, you don't have to fret over the fact that it cost you $10 to $15 and it would be a waste not to finish it. You can just try something else instead, since your drinks are already paid for.

Here's a rundown of select cruise lines offering preorder beverage packages. For current prices and specific details, visit their websites.

- **Azamara Club Cruises**
  (https://www.azamaraclubcruises.com/booked-guests/onboard-packages/beverage-packages)

- **Carnival Cruise Line**
  (https://www.carnival.com/onboard/cheers)

- **Celebrity Cruises**
  (https://www.celebritycruises.com/things-to-do-onboard/onboard-packages/beverage-packages)

- **Costa Cruises**
  (https://www.costacruise.com/usa/all-inclusive-cruise.html)

- **Holland America Line**
  (https://www.hollandamerica.com/en_US.html)

- **Viking Ocean Cruises**
  (https://www.vikingcruises.com)

- **MSC Cruises**
  (https://www.msccruisesusa.com/en-us/Manage-Your-Booking/All-Inclusive-Packages.aspx)

- **Norwegian Cruise Line**
  (https://www.ncl.com/onboard-packages/beverage-packages)

- **Oceania Cruises**
  (https://www.oceaniacruises.com/value/beverage-wine-packages)

- **Princess Cruises**
  (https://www.princess.com/ships-and-experience/food-and-dining/beverages)

- **Royal Caribbean International**
  (https://www.royalcaribbean.com/experience/beverage-packages)

- **Windstar Cruises**
  (https://www.windstarcruises.com/why-windstar/services)

While the idea of paying one large amount for your drinks before your ship sets sail may seem extravagant at first, you'll be glad you did once you realize you have the luxury of being able to order your favorite beverages at most onboard bars and restaurants and not think twice about the bill — not to mention the satisfaction of knowing that you paid much less than the other guy.

INCOME SECRET NO. 26:

Save at Least 85% on Airfare With This Quick, "Old-School" Travel Tip

The price of airfare these days can be outrageous, depending on where you're going and when.

The key word, however, is "can."

It's just as easy to fly anywhere in the world — Cleveland, Ohio; Cancun, Mexico; or Cologne, Germany — at bargain-basement prices.

How? By using a decades-old, yet often forgotten, travel tip.

Even in this digital age with all its integrated travel platforms and supposedly cut-rate, third-party booking websites at your disposal, it is often more advantageous to book your travel arrangements directly through the airline either on their website or by calling them.

Travel writer Akash Gupta recently related his experience booking a flight from Los Angeles to Dallas/Fort Worth wherein the airline's website displayed a round-trip ticket price of just $68 as opposed to the prices ranging from $126 to $176 on various online travel agencies. That's a whopping difference of at *least* 85%!

And guess what? This is also true for hotel accommodations. Even if you find a lower fare or room rate elsewhere, major airlines and hotel chains usually have a "best rate guarantee." Sometimes, they'll even throw in credit vouchers or discounts for use on future bookings too.

While it may be just as convenient to use an online travel agency (OTA) for your travel arrangements, it's also costlier. With an airline or hotel, you don't have to pay additional booking, change or cancellation fees.

Some airlines (e.g., Southwest and Allegiant) don't even bother listing their fares on OTAs, while others (e.g., Lufthansa and British Airways) impose surcharges when you reserve through one instead of through their booking channel. That's how fierce the competition is for your business.

Dealing with airlines and hotels directly also gives you more leverage in case you need to change, delay or cancel your travel arrangements. That's because the reservation is just between two parties — you and the airline or hotel — with no middleman. In fact, some third parties add an additional charge for changing or canceling your flight — on top of the airline's change fee.

Another advantage of booking directly with an airline or hotel is that you can leverage any elite benefits and pile up loyalty points. You can earn frequent flyer miles through an OTA if the fare class is eligible, but most hotel chains do not award points or recognize elite status for your stay if it is booked through a third party.

You can also cash in on special deals or amenities when you work one-on-one with airlines and hotels. These can include additional miles or points, room upgrades, free Wi-Fi, food and beverage credits, special packages, and more that are not available through any third party.

And when you factor in the poor — or at best, mediocre — customer service you might receive from an online travel agency in the event of a discrepancy or an overbooking situation, who needs the aggravation?

Take a tip from the pros and book directly with your airline carrier and hotel of choice. It's cheaper, simpler *and* just as convenient.

INCOME SECRET NO. 27:

Stay 6 Nights in a South Pacific Island Paradise for Less Than $900

When it comes to visiting the tropical islands and coral atolls of the South Pacific, two images come to mind. One is crystal blue waters, palm trees and coral reefs. The other image is how thin your wallet's going to be after you finish paying for the trip.

Visiting an exotic South Pacific island like Vanuatu or Bora Bora is expensive. It costs a lot to fly there and back; there's not much anyone can do about that part. But once you get to these fascinating locales, visitors often find that the accommodations, food, island transportation and entertainment options aren't cheap either.

But veteran travelers say there is one island that the budget-minded among us would be happy to visit: Fiji.

Actually, Fiji, more accurately, is not one island, but an archipelago of 333 palm-fringed islets with names such as Viti Levu, Mamanuca and Yasawa. Only about a third of the islands are inhabited, but there is plenty to explore.

The official languages are Fijian and English. The country has a mix of indigenous, Asian and European cultures and religions, offering travelers a mix of the familiar and the exotic when they visit.

Fiji is the perfect destination no matter the time of year. The tropical island has a year-round temperature of approximately 86 degrees Fahrenheit, while trade winds keep visitors cool. The drier months tend to be May through October, while there is a potential for tropical storms between November and April. Late March through early December tends to be the most popular time for vacationers to visit, while June and July are peak months for tourists.

The main island is Viti Levu, which is where most Fijians live and is home to the capital, Suva. You can travel to the island Nadi where you can visit the Sri Siva Subramaniya Temple or purchase wooden artifacts. Yasawa Island offers a hike through a rainforest or scuba diving around some colorful reefs. Through the months of May to October, you can swim with manta rays around the waters of Nanuya Balavu Island.

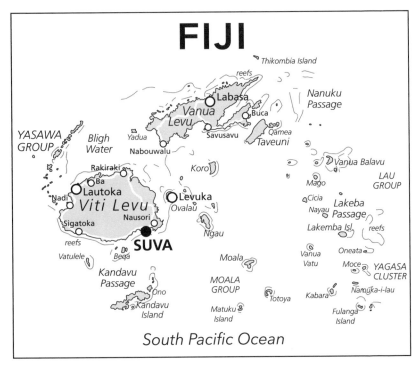

On Fiji, you will find exquisite beaches, rich jungles, colorful reefs, exotic cuisine and a welcoming atmosphere. Upon arriving in Fiji, you will be able to take part in ancient ceremonies, eat traditional foods, go fishing, snorkeling, diving, golfing, shopping, surfing, cycling, horseback riding, jet boating, ziplining, hiking, windsurfing, parasailing, and much, much more.

Or maybe your idea of relaxation is to kick back under an umbrella on the beach with a good book. Well, Fiji can definitely handle that demand as well.

If you love unpretentious opportunities for diving, hiking, rafting and island hopping, Fiji is the place to go.

Just how cheap is it?

As of 2018, you could book a memorable vacation's worth of beachside accommodations, island hopping (and a lifetime of experiences) for as little as $900.

Three-star hotels can be found for as low as $63 per night, while five-star beachfront hotels can be found for as low as $130 per night.

No wonder this island chain is so wildly popular with Aussies and New Zealanders already!

INCOME SECRET NO. 28:

Vacation for Free – as an International House Sitter

What if you could spend a month, a summer or even an entire year in any idyllic getaway of your choice … without spending a dime on a place to stay?

I'm not talking about ramshackle accommodations like some closet-sized spare bedroom, or crashing on a lumpy fold-out couch…

I know, it sounds like a pipe dream. But many people are shocked to discover they can have a luxurious, two-bedroom apartment in London or spacious waterfront cabana in Bermuda all to themselves … for free.

House sitting is a great way for retirees, or anyone for that matter, to spend extended periods of time in dream locations, in beautiful homes, without paying a penny on lodging.

In fact, one Canadian couple — Dalene and Peter Heck, who run their own website called Hecktic Travels — chronicled how they saved more than $30,000 in accommodation costs by house sitting their way around the globe.

All you have to do is keep an eye on someone's home while they're away, and you get to stay in it for free, saving money on accommodations and food expenses since your lodging includes a kitchen. In return, the owners get peace of mind knowing their house is safe. It's a win-win situation.

Another great thing about house-sitting jobs is that they can last anywhere from two weeks to six months, if not longer. That extended stay can enable you to immerse yourself in the local culture and to visit places that regular tourists rarely have the time to cram into their schedule.

How Do You Become a House Sitter?

It's simple: You start by asking family, friends and colleagues about the possibility of watching their home while they're away.

It's a good way to get some experience — and references — under your belt.

Next, you join house-sitting websites. There you can review available listings and apply for house-sitting jobs, carefully choosing them according to your desires based on location, time and other needs.

These websites provide listings for a fee, ranging from $20 to $60 depending on the membership. If you create an account on multiple websites, it can increase your chances of being chosen for a house-sitting job.

Some of the most popular house-sitting websites include:

- TrustedHousesitters
  (https://www.trustedhousesitters.com/us)
- House Sitters America
  (https://www.housesittersamerica.com)
- The Caretaker Gazette
  (http://www.caretaker.org)
- Mind My House
  (https://www.mindmyhouse.com)

Preparing Your Application

Once you join a house-sitting website, create a profile that emphasizes the following:

- Your experience as a house-sitter or a previous homeowner;
- Your fondness for pets (house sitting often involves pet sitting as well);
- Any special skills you have, such as speaking a foreign language or being handy with tools or gardening; and your enthusiasm for the job.

While reviewing available listings, be flexible in your plans and throw as wide a net as possible.

Also, check out Visa requirements for countries you plan to apply for since many countries — including at least two dozen in Europe — only allow Americans to stay up to 90 days at a time.

Then strike while the iron is hot. When a house-sitting opportunity is posted, try to apply within minutes since attractive house sites go fast. To be able to act quickly, sign up for email alerts in your desired area. Pay close attention to the listing and draft an email according to specific details in that listing.

When applying for a house-sitting gig, be sure to provide references. It helps to have quality people who'll vouch for you, such as former landlords, previous neighbors, ex-bosses or anyone who can attest to your character, reliability and trustworthiness.

It's also important to know as much as possible about the residence and folks who are entrusting you with their house keys to avoid any inconvenient or unpleasant surprises. So, ask a lot of pertinent questions before you arrive, such as:

- Are you allowed to have visitors?
- Can you leave the property overnight?
- Will there be a vehicle available for local transportation?
- Is there a home security system? If so, what is the activation code?
- Will there be internet service? Wi-Fi? Is there a password?

House sitting is a great way to see the world without technically leaving home. And think of the hundreds — or thousands — of dollars you'll save!

INCOME SECRET NO. 29:

Get a 200% Retirement
"Pay Raise" for Taking a Trip

Rest and relaxation aren't the only reasons the wealthy love to travel. Too often, we dream of living, only part time in these amazing locations. However, we have convinced ourselves that some places are so beautiful they must be more expensive than where we are currently living.

But the truth is that an idyllic summer getaway could double the value of your retirement!

Rent, restaurants and grocery costs are up to 55% lower in countries such as Portugal, Costa Rica and Spain. This means every dollar of retirement income will give you DOUBLE the purchasing power … e.g., last twice as long as would in the U.S.

Most tourists who only spend a week in such places won't really see/feel this boost in savings.

But folks who stay longer term, say three to six months, will save tons on rent and food.

And they can even rent out their house back in the United States while they're gone to cover what oversees living costs they do have.

Easy to say, almost impossible to achieve, right?

Suddenly, the "impossible" isn't so impossible after all. Just take a look at the chart on the next page, looking at six categories of living expenses (food, housing, transportation, personal care, entertainment and cost vs. U.S.) in a variety of sunny offshore retirement locales.

Country	Food	Rent	Trans.	Personal Care	Entmnt.	Cost vs U.S.
Punta del Este, Uruguay	-24%	-50%	-49%	-35%	-12%	-35%
Granada, Nicaragua	-46%	-32%	-17%	-20%	-34%	-30%
Panama City, Panama	-9%	-13%	-44%	-29%	-2%	-18%
Seville, Spain	-28%	-41%	-20%	-24%	-32%	-30%
Lisbon, Portugal	-31%	-42%	-3%	-36%	-13%	-25%
Source: Expatistan						

In other words, moving offshore is like giving yourself a large jump in income, simply because prices in these locations (and many others) are so much cheaper, and your money goes so much further in value.

You can take this one step further and buy your own place overseas. The prices vary, depending on the country in question, foreign exchange rates and the property's location (beachside, mountains, urban, etc.), but it's something that most people should at least take a look at when considering their retirement options.

Some people buy a place, live in it part-time and rent it out (with the help of a real estate management firm) for a number of months. Others buy a place and make it their full-time residence.

It should not come as a surprise that the United States isn't the most inexpensive place to live. There are actually a number of amazing places around the globe that have a lower cost of living — allowing you to easily stretch your nest egg even further — while adding a sense of adventure and discovery to your retirement.

INCOME SECRET NO. 30:

Summer in a Dream Vacation Spot for Free — and Earn Money Doing It

Returning home from a vacation can be really tough. There's usually a five-stage cycle after unpacking your things.

First comes telling anyone who will listen — and some who won't — about the amazing cuisine and culture you experienced abroad.

Next, you find yourself in a staff meeting or stuck in traffic, daydreaming about quitting your job and selling everything to move to your dream destination.

After that comes some research to check out that country's job market and housing prices. Then, reality sets in: You think you can't afford a drastic lifestyle change after all. The best you can do is settle for planning your next trip (as soon as you've accrued enough time off work), instead of living a "permanent vacation" lifestyle in the overseas destination of your choice.

But what if the post-vacation cycle didn't have to end that way?

What if there was an affordable way to acquire a second citizenship, buy property in your favorite Caribbean island or Latin American getaway and rent it out to cover all the costs when you're not using it?

That's the idea behind this Income Secret. You can do it and enjoy the privileges that come with dual citizenship ... and a retirement rental property that pays its own way.

After all, people do this all the time with vacation properties located inside the U.S. ... but there's nothing stopping you from doing it abroad too.

Now may be the best time to make this investment in your future. Not only are you creating a retirement haven for your later years, but you're also creating a safe haven for yourself in the event of turmoil or economic unrest at home. And with the strength of the U.S. dollar, there's no better time to buy overseas.

Choosing a Country

If you've spent some time exploring the world, you may already have a pretty good idea of where you'd like to spend more time. Perhaps it's the ocean breezes and laidback lifestyle that lures you back to your apartment in Montevideo, or your getaway on the Caribbean island of Grenada each year or the architecture and culture of Italy that make you feel relaxed, like you're visiting a simpler time.

But before you make an emotional decision, consider the practical issues:

1. **Restrictions on foreign ownership:** Not all countries allow foreigners to own property outright. This is obviously important when you purchase property for the first time, but it could also be critical if and when you decide to sell it to realize its value. Unrestricted foreign ownership rights mean you're operating in a global market, not just a national one. You can sell to other foreigners as well as locals.

2. **Market stability and liquidity:** Obviously, you want to invest in places that will maintain the conditions that prompted you to buy there in the first place. It's impossible to predict the future, but there are many countries that can boast decades of stability on the issues that matter — property rights, taxation, openness to foreigners and so on. That's where you want to invest in property. But you also want to be sure that you can liquidate your property holdings when the time comes, so choosing a country with an active property market is important too. The good news is that the two factors — stability and liquidity — tend to go hand-in-hand.

3. **Title security:** Some countries with seemingly attractive upfront property deals also have weak titling and deeds registry systems. This can come back to haunt you if someone comes along with a stack of old paperwork and claims that your land was actually stolen from his grandfather. Even if it isn't true, it can tie your property up for years.

4. **Buying costs:** Every country levies some form of tax or duty at the time of a real estate transaction, which is usually shared by buyer and seller. It's important to anticipate this cost so you can balance it against expected land value appreciation and other cost factors.

5. **Property tax:** Some countries don't levy any property tax. But most do, and like transaction taxes, these need to be taken into account when working out how much of your wealth you're going to be preserving, and how much you're going to be giving to the foreign taxman for the privilege.

6. **Capital gains tax:** Capital gains taxes on property sales vary widely. Some countries don't levy any at all, or tax it as ordinary income. But some — including some of the most popular expat destinations — have capital gains rates in the double-digits. You want to know up front if you're going to be trading low transaction and property taxes now for big capital gains hit when you sell and vice versa. But bear in mind that the IRS is going to tax you on any gains from foreign property sales — so the most important thing is to ensure that the foreign rate is below or equal to U.S. rates — which are 15% to 20% for most households. That way, you can deduct the foreign capital gains tax from your U.S. tax obligations and come out even. If you invest in a country with a capital gains rate above the U.S., you will pay more in taxes.

7. **Choosing the right property agent:** In many countries, the real estate agent sets the sale price, not the property owner. The seller specifies the minimum amount they want from the sale, but the agent tries to sell for a lot more to make a profit. There's often no U.S.-style multiple listing service that allows you to compare what different agents might be asking. So it's important to seek out trustworthy agents and advisers who can help you understand the local property market, values and opportunities.

Country	Foreign Ownership Restrictions	Title Security	Average Buying Costs	Property Tax	Capital Gains Tax	Stability
Belize	None	Medium	6.5%	1.00%	0%	High
Cayman Islands	None	High	7.5%	0.00%	0%	High
Costa Rica	Minor	High	5.0%	0.25%	0%	High
Dominica	Minor	High	21.0%	0.00%	0%	High
Dominican Republic	None	Medium	5.0%	1.00%	29%	High
Ecuador	Coastal	Medium	3.0%	0.25%	35%	Medium
Malta	Minor	High	12.0%	0.00%	0%	High
Mexico	Coastal	High	3.0%	0.28%	30%	High
Nicaragua	None	Medium	6.5%	0.25%	20%	High
Panama	Minor	High	2.3%	2.10%	10%	High
Turks & Caicos	None	High	10.0%	0.00%	0%	High
Uruguay	None	High	8.0%	0.25%	12%	High

For a variety of reasons, the Caribbean and certain parts of Latin America have distinct advantages for Americans compared to other regions around the world. For instance, the Caribbean islands (as well as Central American countries like Panama, Costa Rica and Nicaragua) have relatively short travel times from U.S. airports, in terms of hours spent in the air, and therefore closer for your friends and family to come for visits and vice versa.

The one downside of Latin America, however, is the language. You may already speak Spanish or have a knack for picking up the local lingo and adjusting quickly to living in a new culture. If you don't, you may feel isolated and feel like you've made a mistake — although most locals are very tolerant of language issues. Everyone is different when it comes to these kinds of questions and the only person who can provide the honest answer is you.

Paths to Citizenship

Once you've zeroed in on a dream destination for your second home abroad, you may want to consider what it would take to acquire citizenship there someday. A second passport gives the right of residence as well as all the protections of being subject to a foreign government. Second passports are especially handy for those who want to be able to use that document to get around the visa requirements imposed on their compatriots while traveling. Of course, it also provides an escape route to a friendlier clime should the need arise.

- **Economic citizenship:** The fastest way to obtain a second passport — but certainly not the cheapest — is through an economic citizenship program, where you essentially buy a second citizenship. These programs often take the form of an investment program where you either invest in real estate or in certain funds as specified by the local government.

  One well-known program is the island country of St. Kitts and Nevis, where you make an investment in the country and in return get a St. Kitts passport and citizenship. You have two options: Either invest $400,000 in qualified real estate or donate a nonrefundable amount of $250,000 to the Sugar Industry Diversification Foundation. You'll enjoy visa-free access to 120 countries, including the U.K., Hong Kong, Schengen and Singapore. This route is also available in Antigua, Barbuda, Dominica and Grenada.

  None of these citizenships are automatic; all involve a due diligence process and subjective evaluation by an immigration board. Aside from the fee imposed on individuals, couples or families, there are also government fees and agency fees to factor in. Some countries, such as Antigua and Barbuda, have a residence requirement and others, like Dominica, have an interview process.

- **Naturalization:** There are far cheaper dual citizenships to go after if you're willing to wait out the naturalization period. This usually involves a specific period of prior residence in the country and/or marriage to a citizen. Almost all countries have a route to obtain permanent residence, often linked to marriage, a job, starting a business or other commitments to the country. But this means actually living in the country for a period — usually five years — before acquiring citizenship. Note that marriage to a citizen does not always confer automatic residence.

- **Sanguinity:** This option is available by descent or other affinity to the national community (e.g., religion). The most common is for people born in the U.S. to parents from a foreign country, who often acquire that citizenship automatically. Some countries give citizenship to foreigners descended from at least one grandparent (sometimes further back) from that country. Countries that offer this route include: Italy, Greece, Turkey, Bulgaria, Lebanon, Armenia, Romania, Afghanistan, the Philippines, Croatia, Estonia, Hungary, Ireland, Israel, Lithuania, Malta, Poland, Rwanda, Serbia, Slovakia, South Korea and Ukraine.

Economic Citizenship at a Glance				
	Dominica	St. Kitts/ Nevis	Antigua/ Barbuda	Grenada
Fee (individual)	$100,000	$250,000	$200,000	n/a
Fee (couple)	$175,000	$300,000	$200,000	n/a
Government Fees	Procedural fees of $1,765; due diligence fees of $4,000	$50,000 for applicant; due diligence fees of $15,000	$50,000 (investment option only)	Included for main applicant, $5,350 for spouse
Agency Fees	$20,000	$25,000	$45,000 plus due diligence costs	Unknown
Residence Requirement	None	None	Five days over five years	None
Interview	Yes	No	No	No
Visa-free Access	90 countries (U.K., Switzerland, HK, Singapore)	120 countries (U.K., HK, Singapore)	139 countries (U.K., Canada, EU, HK, Singapore)	110 countries (U.K., HK, Singapore)

Important Factors to Consider
for Your Overseas Vacation Property

Once you've narrowed down your choice of countries, you're ready to make your real estate decision. Of course, it isn't quite that easy. Let's explore some of the immediate considerations, some of which will seem foreign if you're used to only handling stateside residential real estate transactions.

1. When buying foreign real estate, make sure you know the rules and laws governing foreign ownership of the specific land you want, since they often vary within the country — say near coasts or borders, as in Mexico or Ecuador. If foreign ownership limits are an issue, always get a written guarantee from the authorities.

2. Also, you'll want to make sure you can use your property for your intended purpose. This includes such things as "build requirements." If you're buying a residential lot, you may have to build a home within a certain time frame of months or years. Check the style of house you're allowed to build, the height, size and any other rules you'll have to comply with. In some countries foreigners have to build a house of a certain size and value within a relatively short time of buying a lot.

3. Make sure you research as much as possible about your intended usage of the land. For instance, if you're buying land that you intend on renting out as a farm or ranching property, get an expert to carry out a soil analysis test and give you a full report on its condition and local rainfall patterns. Also, whether the usage you have in mind is appropriate to what the soil and topography of the property can support. Sometimes there are restrictions on the use of property; get your attorney to check the deed with the local municipality.

4. You'll also want to consider infrastructure — your connections for electricity, fresh water, sewer and the internet. Check out the standard of the water supply and sewage treatment systems. Ask if they comply with local regulations. If the land doesn't have access to water or

sewage, figure out how much it will cost to install them. Find out how reliable the electricity supply is — will you need a back-up generator? If you need to install it, how much will that cost and how long will it take? If you want cable, high-speed internet or cell coverage, make sure you can get it on your property.

5. What about road access to your property? If access is via a right-of-way, make sure that it's recorded in the deed. And investigate to see if anyone else has access to your land. If they've used it to get from Point A to Point B or lived on it for long enough, they may have acquired legal rights to carry on doing so.

6. Property boundaries are another important area you'll want to research. Get a proper survey done to establish the legally recognized boundaries of your land. The survey will tell you exactly how much land you're getting. That's very important if you're buying a big parcel of land and paying a price per acre. You need to know you're getting all the acres you're paying for.

Financial Considerations of Renting Your Offshore Property

There's more to think about than just the purchase price of a property. If you want to rent it out — for example, to finance you own annual vacation and/or eventual retirement there — you'll want to make sure you cover all your bases. There are important considerations when it comes to properly handling your offshore real-estate:

- **Hiring a management company** — It's important to get a handle on the yearly expenses in relation to the property, including management fees. It's important to have a person or company on the ground that can deal with maintenance issues while you're hundreds or thousands of miles away. These companies' services can vary, so it's important to choose a really competent and trustworthy real estate management company and manage the relationship the correct way.

- **Banking and income taxes** — If you earn any rental income from your property, it must be reported on your personal U.S. income tax return (Form 1040, Schedule E), regardless of the amount and regardless of whether you are required to report the existence of the property itself to the IRS. If you open a foreign bank account to facilitate the purchase of the property — or to receive rental income and that account has more than $10,000 in it on any one day of the year — then you also must report the bank account to the government, commonly referred to as the Foreign Bank Account Report (FBAR).

- **Double taxation** — When operating your home abroad as a rental property, you will owe taxes in the country where the property is located. To avoid double taxation, you can take a tax credit on your U.S. tax return for any taxes you paid to the foreign country, relating to the net rental income. Bear in mind that you can't take a credit for more than the amount of U.S. tax on the rental income, after deducting expenses, but you're allowed to claim a foreign tax credit if you sell your property and pay capital gains tax in the foreign country.

- **Additional taxes and fees** — You'll likely be faced with some other expenses you hadn't bargained on before all is said and done. For instance, for real estate in St. Kitts, a buyer needs to pay something called a stamp tax, which is 12% of the cost of the property. In Antigua, the stamp tax is about 7%. Depending on how you purchase a property, either through a company or individually, these taxes can go up or down. You'll also want to think about attorney fees. In most common law countries (British-based law), attorneys charge a percentage of the cost of the property in order to do the legal work related to transfer of title (in the U.S., this is called the closing legal fees), which can be up to 2.5% of the cost of the property. These details simply work differently in different countries, so it's important to get a handle on them in advance to avoid ugly surprises.

Foreign-property ownership and tax laws are complicated and change suddenly, so it's wise to consult with a qualified tax accountant and/or real estate attorney both abroad and in the United States.

My Favorite Areas

As you've probably realized by now, you have a wide array of choices for your offshore haven. It all depends on the many variables that have been presented. I have some long-held favorites I'll detail below:

Uruguay: The South American nation of Uruguay is increasingly popular as a destination for foreign property investment. It's a longer flight from the United States, true, but there's a reason that this nation has long been called the Switzerland of the continent. Land prices have been climbing higher over the years, due to the country's many attractive attributes for expat real estate ownership: a strong, stable government, the well-established rule of law and international ownership of property is welcomed and respected. The country also has a mild climate, ample annual rainfall and attractive pieces of farm, ranch and urban real estate to consider for purchase.

Panama: Panama, like Uruguay, has a strong tradition of respect for liberty, property and privacy. Its strong economy is based on its service sector, such as Panama Canal operations and the Colón Free Trade Zone (second only to Hong Kong in trade volume). It's also a key offshore financial center and is an excellent place to consider for your asset protection options as well. As far as "welcoming" goes, two years ago Panama created a new category — "Immediate Permanent Resident" — aimed at attracting foreign nationals. This fast-track program targets professionals, managers and business entrepreneurs. By all accounts, the country is one of the best places to live in the Western Hemisphere. If you love beaches, watersports and tropical landscapes, Panama has all that and more.

AROUND
THE HOUSE

Great sources of potential income and cost-cutting ideas don't have to be limited to your investments and retirement planning strategies. There are plenty of amazing opportunities to increase your savings around your own home. From making smarter decisions with your brand-name prescriptions to taking advantage of the cash-back rewards to attending a class that could potentially trim up to 15% off your auto insurance to making money off the clutter you're already planning to clear out, there are several overlooked options that could put money back into your pocket.

INCOME SECRET NO. 31:

Save 85% on leading Brand-Name Prescriptions

The global pharmaceutical business is pretty messed up, as I am sure you would agree. The prices we pay here in the United States are many times over what people pay abroad for the same medication.

Why is that? A lot of it has to do with how drug companies try to make back the billions they spend in developing new drugs, regulations and, of course, the money they hope to make for their shareholders.

That means different prices for different buyers, so many drug buyers in the "rich world" countries pay more as a result. Even Canada is much cheaper!

But that doesn't mean you have to pay the full cost for every drug your doctor prescribes — or even buy a drug at all.

Start with your doctor, right at the moment he writes the Rx. Ask him: Is this drug really the only solution to my problem? It's counterintuitive, but many of our modern ailments are "solved" by drug consumption, but aren't necessarily "cured."

Take heartburn medications. Would a change in diet mean less need for heartburn meds? Would losing 10 pounds or quitting coffee reduce or eliminate the need for a costly drug? Would moderate, daily exercise offset your need for a pricy blood-pressure med, with all of its side effects?

Join These "Secret Health Savings Clubs"

Wouldn't it be nice if shopping for health care was like shopping for so many other products and services — the kind that come with price discounts? I mean, when was the last time your doctor, dentist, pharmacist or hospital said: "We're having a 20% off sale this month"?

Believe it or not, it's possible to get just such discounts with little-known health savings clubs. Usually you'll find them marketed as "health discount programs." But first, let's get a couple things straight…

- Health discount programs are NOT health insurance.

- There's no reimbursement of your health care providers, either. You get the discount when you pay for the service or product in question.

- You pay a monthly premium, and in return, the administrator of the health discount program negotiates with your doctor and other health care providers to accept a reduced fee.

Why would a doctor or hospital perform agree to that? Because the health discount program brings them an increase in business, in the same way that coupons help cereal and other items fly off your local grocery's shelves.

You can usually save up to 20% to 30% on a provider's services. (But beware any health discount program claiming to offer discounts of 50% or more — chances are it's either a scam, or just plain lying about the real savings you might get from the plan.)

So where can you find a good health discount program? Chances are, if you have a health insurance plan already, then your provider may offer a discount program too. Call up their customer service agents and ask, or look through the plan's guidebook sent to you when you signed up for the policy.

What if you don't have health insurance (or your provider doesn't offer a discount program)?

First, DO NOT buy a health discount program over the internet without doing a lot of research. The Federal Trade Commission warns that while some medical discount plans provide legitimate discounts, others take your money and offer very little in return.

Experts say the right way to find a health discount program is to first visit your personal physician's office and talk to a responsible person in the office's billing unit. Or if you've done some internet research already, and are interested in a particular company's health discount program, bring the sales pamphlet or printouts with you to the doctor's office.

The billing person there will be able to advise you on the discount plan, whether its provider is legitimate or not, and whether you can get the advertised discounts from the doctor's office.

Yes, it takes a little extra work, but it's well worth it when you consider the savings involved on just a few visits to a doctor (dentists, hospitals, pharmacists and other health care providers, too).

Save 85% With Generics

If you must take a drug, absolutely ask for generic options first. Generic drugs are identical to their name-brand versions and can be up to 85% cheaper. If you have a very high insurance deductible, you will pay out-of-pocket 100%, so make sure to get generics whenever possible.

Your cost of coinsurance will be lower, too, on generic drugs. You are likely to pay coinsurance equal to 50% of the cost of a branded drug, but as low as 10% of the cost of a cheaper generic alternative.

The insurance company will also steer you toward these lower cost options — choices which might not be obvious until you ask.

Doctors prescribe non-generics out of habit, or because they have been sweet-talked by a "pill pusher" from the drug's maker. The visiting salesperson showers the office with coffee and donuts and plies doctors with free travel to "conferences" in tropical locations.

It's your money, so push back. Tell the doctor you want generics in every case possible and get their honest reaction.

You are likely to find, too, that your insurer simply won't pay for some name-brand prescriptions at all because of the high cost. In this case, be sure to ask your doctor if using the name brand is absolutely crucial.

He might cite reasons why the name brand is preferred — reasons you might agree with. In all other cases, generics will be fine, and you will save big just by switching.

Grab Deep Rx Discounts

Don't stop there. Big-box retail chains such as Walmart, Target and the warehouse stores typically offer volume pricing on generic drugs.

If you know you will take a specific medication for a long time, you can find them in these pharmacies much cheaper than at your normal corner drugstore. Discount stores are up to 60% cheaper for commonly prescribed drugs for cholesterol, high blood pressure and other chronic ailments.

Your insurance company also may have a deal to drive your business to Costco or a similar warehouse store where you already shop. Low-cost drugs are a "loss leader" for them — a way to get people into the store.

Don't Pay the "Convenience Markup"

Another way to look at it: Using a "non-preferred" drugstore is probably going to cost more for the same drug — sometimes much more. Most people just go to the drugstore on the way home from their doctor's office.

They unwittingly pay a premium for that convenience.

It's the difference between buying milk at a gas station versus at a grocery store. Which do you think will be more expensive? The faster and more convenient option, for sure.

Don't go from the doctor's office straight to buy your prescription, unless your physician instructs you to do so. Go home, fire up the internet and research prices first.

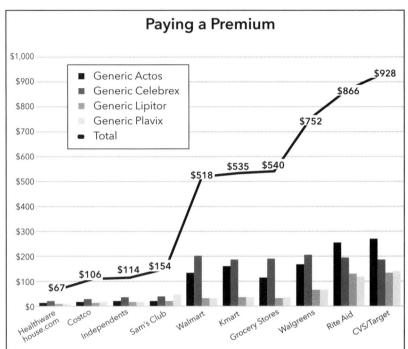

Paying a Premium

The prices for a 30-day supply of five commonly prescribed generic drugs varied widely in this survey of online and drugstore sources. The black line shows the total monthly cost if you bought all five at the corresponding stores below.

SOURCE: Consumer Reports

If you know you're going to take a drug for the long term and you have to start it right away, go ahead and buy that first month's supply. But then look into pharmacies by mail, where prices for a 90-day supply are often the same as the cost for just 30 days' supply at the corner chain drugstore. Many insurers have special relationships with pharmacies by mail or through a "preferred" pharmacy.

Be an Online Sleuth

Remember, many of your friends and neighbors likely already take advantage of these price breaks. Ask around! The drugstores have no incentive to advertise lower prices, nor do the drug companies.

Your doctor won't even bring it up. So you have to do some sleuthing to find the best price, particularly if you expect to take a drug for a long period of time.

If you do end up taking a name-brand drug, set up a Google alert online for the drug's brand name, plus the words "generic" or "patent expiration."

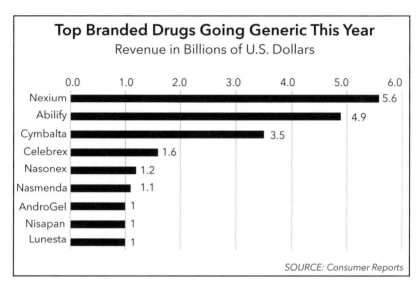

Top Branded Drugs Going Generic This Year
Revenue in Billions of U.S. Dollars

Nexium	5.6
Abilify	4.9
Cymbalta	3.5
Celebrex	1.6
Nasonex	1.2
Nasmenda	1.1
AndroGel	1
Nisapan	1
Lunesta	1

SOURCE: Consumer Reports

Many drugs have a specific window of time before they are forced to release the drug's formulation to generic providers. Go to www.google.com/alerts and follow the simple instructions there. You will get emails daily or weekly as news stories feature your chosen keywords.

Your costly prescription drug might be on the verge of dropping in price!

Some insurers, too, will send you email alerts on your meds, precisely to tell you when prices fall, but you have to set that up online, too. Check with your provider.

INCOME SECRET NO. 32:

Switch to a Cash-Back Rewards Gas Credit Card

Gas prices are once again on the rise. As each trip to the pump threatens to take a bigger bite out of your wallet, it's time to take back a little more of your money.

If you haven't done so already, consider applying for a gas-company credit card that offers cash-back rebates with your purchases. You can save up to $600 per year on this kind of program.

For example, BP has a loyalty rewards program called BP Driver Rewards. It allows customers to earn at a rate of $0.10 off per gallon for every $100 spent on BP fuel. Not only that, you have the option to earn those rewards in the form of cents off per gallon at BP or United MileagePlus® award miles.

For your added convenience, you can link your BP Driver Rewards account to your qualified debit or credit card and automatically earn and use fuel rewards or MileagePlus miles every time you swipe your card at a BP gas pump.

But that's not all! If you do choose award miles, you'll earn up to 3 MileagePlus miles with every gallon of BP gas you purchase. In addition, you'll earn 200 bonus miles for making your first transaction after linking your card.

For more details about the BP Driver Rewards program or to join, visit https://www.mybpstation.com/bp-driver-rewards.

Other gas companies such as Shell and Speedway offer similar rebate programs. For example, Shell Fuel Rewards members earn $0.05 per gallon for every $25 spent inside participating Shell stations. Whether it's a cup of coffee or a car wash, they earn Fuel Rewards® savings on specially marked items, plus they save up to $0.10 per gallon for every fill-up with Shell V-Power® NiTRO+ Premium Gasoline. For more details or to participate, visit https://www.fuelrewards.com/fuelrewards.

Meanwhile, Speedway Speedy Rewards members earn 20 points per dollar on in-store purchases and 10 points per gallon on their fuel purchases. These points can be redeemed for free featured items such as food, beverages, fuel discounts and gift cards using Speedway's mobile app. For more information, visit https://www.speedway.com/SpeedyRewards.

If you depend on personal transportation, cash-back programs are a great way to fill up your tank and get rewarded for your customer loyalty.

INCOME SECRET NO. 33:

Save 15% on Auto Insurance by Taking This Course

Sick of paying high auto insurance premiums — especially when you've never had an accident?

Then enroll in a defensive driving safety course to save up to 15% on your auto insurance.

If 15% doesn't sound like a significant savings, do the math: For every $1,000 per year you spend on auto insurance, you could be saving $150. Depending on where you live and your previous driving record, that could mean savings of anywhere from $150 to $450 or more ... every year you drive.

Defensive driving classes are often sponsored by groups such as AARP, AAA and the Safety Council to promote better motoring skills — and therefore less risk of accidents — among both older and younger drivers. These courses, which can be conducted in a classroom or online, usually range in cost from $15 to $100, but are worth the investment.

According to AARP: "By taking a driver refresher course you'll learn the current rules of the road, defensive driving techniques and how to operate your vehicle more safely in today's increasingly challenging driving environment. And you'll learn how you can manage and accommodate common age-related changes in vision, hearing and reaction time."

Currently, 34 states and Washington, D.C., mandate a discount for safe-driving classes. These states include Alabama, Alaska, Arkansas, California, Colorado, Connecticut, Delaware, Florida, Georgia, Idaho, Illinois, Kansas, Kentucky, Louisiana, Maine, Minnesota, Mississippi, Montana, Nevada, New Jersey, New Mexico, New York, North Dakota, Oklahoma, Oregon, Pennsylvania, Rhode Island, South Carolina, Tennessee, Utah, Virginia, Washington, West Virginia and Wyoming.

The mandated discounts cover all drivers who take the courses, regardless of their age, with the exception of New Mexico, which prohibits the discount for drivers under 50.

However, some but not all insurers in non-mandated states offer discounts for course participation, according to the Insurance Information Institute.

Also, some state-mandated insurers do not accept online classes, so you should speak with your insurance company or agent before signing up for a defensive driving course to verify whether you can get credit for taking an online class and find out how much of a discount you can expect.

Age requirements can vary from state to state and among insurers. For example, Esurance requires older drivers to be at least 55, while Allstate offers a safe driver discount for those older than 50. Meanwhile, some insurers offer discounts for those 25 and younger, while others reserve the discount for those 21 and below.

Here's a rundown of what some of the major insurers offer (depending on the state) for both older and younger drivers who take a defensive driving class, according to company representatives and the insurer's website:

- Farmers Insurance — About a 10% discount for older drivers and up to 10% for younger drivers.

- State Farm — Up to 10% for both older and younger drivers.

- Nationwide — About 5% for both older and younger drivers.

- Esurance — About 5% for older drivers and up to 15% for younger drivers.

- Geico — About 5% for both older and younger drivers.

- Allstate and The Hartford — Up to 10% for all drivers, any age.

- Liberty Mutual, Progressive and USAA — About 5% for both older and younger drivers.

Besides saving you money on your insurance premiums, a defensive driving course could also result in a reduction of points on your driver's license and waiver of a fine following a driving violation ticket.

But best of all, it'll help make you a better driver and safer on the road.

INCOME SECRET NO. 34:

Earn up to $10,000 Per Year
Renting Out Your Own Car

Owning a car can be as expensive as having another dependent. You need to buy or finance it. Then, of course, there are insurance premiums, the expense of maintaining and repairing the car, and then paying out hundreds of dollars or more per year just to keep the tank full.

But what if your car could earn its keep … in other words, pay *you*?

Renting out your car using apps such as Turo, Hyre or Getaround can earn you up to $10,000 or more per year in extra income. With that additional income, you could pay off the cost of your car in as little as two years, invest the money, help pay a child's college tuition, boost your retirement nest egg or spend it as you wish.

Here's how car-sharing typically works:

When you list your car on Turo, you decide how many days per month you want to rent it out. The higher the market value of your vehicle and the number of days you choose to rent it out, the more money you can make. For example, if your car's market value is $20,000 and you choose to rent it out for just 10 days per month, you could earn $4,664.

Turo will set your car's rental price based on market value, location, time of the year and other data set to maximize your income and boost your listing's competitiveness. Or, if you prefer, you can manually set your own daily price, as well as the mileage limit.

Turo will pay you by direct deposit within five business days. You'll earn 65% to 85% of the rental price, depending on the vehicle protection package you have chosen. If you already have commercial rental insurance that covers you, your car and your customers, you have the option of waiving the vehicle protection provided by Turo, thus earning 90% of the rental price.

The vehicle protection provided by Turo includes $1 million in liability insurance, and your car is also covered against theft and physical damage. In addition, your car is returned to you refueled.

Hyre and Getaround have similar terms and conditions, although rental prices and earnings may vary. However, listing your vehicle on any of these car-sharing services is totally free with no monthly fees and no buy-ins.

For more details, visit https://turo.com, https://www.hyrecar.com or https://www.getaround.com and start putting your car to work for you.

INCOME SECRET NO. 35:

Review Your Auto Insurance Bill to Save $531

We've all seen the commercials telling us to shop around for a better rate because we may be paying more than necessary with our current carrier. And in some cases, it can be true.

According to the Federal Consumer Price Index, car insurance rates usually rise an average of 3% to 4% per year, but rates have been jumping faster in recent years. In December 2016, care insurance rates shot up 7% from the same time a year earlier.

In 2017, car insurance rate soared 7.9%.

Advances in safety and technology within cars have resulted in a steeper price increase over the past several years. Even if you haven't gotten a new, more advanced car, you might have seen your insurance increase with everyone else's.

So, it's best to at least shop around to see if you're getting the best rate possible. A couple of phone calls or web searches can really pay off.

For example, if you or your spouse are 50 years of age or over, requesting a rate quote request from AARP® Auto Insurance Program from The Hartford may prove very fruitful. This insurer offers competitive rates that are worth investigating that may reward you with significant savings.

Also, an auto insurance policy through AAA can save members an average of $531 per year. Please visit your local AAA website or office for further details.

Some other tips for lowering your auto insurance include:

1. **Bundle your policies.** If you get your car insurance from the same company that offers homeowners or renters insurance, you can possibly save up to 25% on each policy from some companies.

2. **Purchase a cheaper car.** Consider a pre-owned car without the advanced gadgets such as backup cameras. Older cars are also less risky for insurers because they are less expensive to replace. If you car's value is less than 10 times the premium, you may want to reduce or drop your collision and/or comprehensive coverage, as well.

3. **Pay your bills on time.** A low credit score often results in higher car insurance. Paying your bills on time will improve your credit score and lower your car insurance payment. You may also be able to get a discount if you choose auto-billing and if you pay for a full year upfront versus paying month-by-month.

INCOME SECRET NO. 36:

Chop Your Cable Cord ... and Save Big

"Not wasting money is just as important as making money in any prudent investment strategy," I'd said in my presentation at the Offshore Investment Summit.

Out of the corner of my eye I saw a little man's head snap up, his eyes fixed on me. He'd been taking notes up to then, head bowed to the table. But from that moment onward he stared at me in rapt attention.

After I was done — my session was just before the afternoon coffee break — he cornered me on my way out of the hall.

Uh-oh, I thought. No coffee for me. I had to be back onstage to introduce the panel discussion in 15 minutes.

"Until you spoke, I was worried that nobody really understood the secret of wealth," he said, in a thick Swiss-German accent. "But you clearly do." I nodded politely, the smell of fresh coffee and leche tugging at my nostrils. "What you just said is the wisdom of the ages, as far as I am concerned."

"You mean the part about not trusting any politician who isn't Uruguayan?" I ventured. Instantly I recognized my father's brand of irreverent humor, albeit unsure of its appropriateness in conversation.

The apple doesn't fall far from tree, for better and worse.

The little man looked right past my quip in the way that only the Swiss can do.

"No, I mean about not wasting money as the key to wealth."

Free Your Mind, Then Your Wallet

Okay, then ... I know a bit about that! After all, I spent the bulk of my career working in the nonprofit sector, where salaries are nothing to write home about.

But my interest in good value and savings goes beyond dollars and cents. I see it as a critical aspect of my more general passion ... to live as freely as possible and to escape traps laid for me by the powers that be, and to help others to do the same.

The problem is that in today's America, mainstream media and pundits — all working for big private corporations — strongly encourage us to focus our discontent on government and politicians. And they certainly deserve a lot of that! But a mono-focus on Washington distracts us from problems that are at least as important as an out-of-control government.

Thanks, perhaps, to my many years spent outside the U.S., I see the country from a slightly different perspective; one that is also sensitive to the ways in which accumulations of power outside government also shape our fortunes in negative ways.

For example, I know for a fact that on a like-for-like basis, I pay a great deal more for my broadband internet service in the U.S. than I would if I lived in any other developed country, as well as a number of less-developed countries. The same is true for health care, education and other crucial services. The reason for this? As *The Economist* puts it:

> *One problem with American capitalism has been overlooked: a corrosive lack of competition. The naughty secret of American firms is that life at home is much easier: their returns on equity are 40% higher in the United States than they are abroad. Aggregate domestic profits are at near record levels relative to GDP. America is meant to be a temple of free enterprise. It isn't.*

An average 40% return on equity is unheard of in economic history. An individual firm may be capable of sustained returns like that for a while, but would expect to see their profits "competed away" eventually. Today, however, a very profitable American firm has an 80% chance of being that way 10 years later. In the 1990s, the odds were only about 50%.

The problem is that steep corporate earnings aren't luring in new entrants because established firms are abusing monopoly positions, or using lobbying to stifle competition. Indeed, two-thirds of the U.S. economy's 900-odd industries have become more concentrated since 1997. A tenth of the economy is at the mercy of a handful of firms. At the same time, the rate of small-company creation in America is close to its lowest mark ever.

What are we to do about this if our politicians won't do anything? Well, you can't "vote the b******s out" when they are private corporations, industry associations or lobbyists. The best way I can think of to fight back is to explore the ways they rip us off, and how to stop that from happening by adopting smart, little-known techniques to avoid doing business with them altogether.

Cable: How (and Why) They're Ripping You Off

For most of us, television in the first half of our lives meant tuning into the broadcast networks, CBS, ABC and NBC, and enduring commercials (and poor reception) as the price of free entertainment.

All that changed with the rapid spread of cable TV in the 1980s. By the end of the decade, there were about 30 channels available on most cable networks. By the mid-90s the numbers had exploded into the hundreds — cable's vastly greater bandwidth made that technically feasible.

This plethora of content led to the development of "tiered" cable offerings, in which a higher monthly subscription fee gave you more channels to watch. The trick was that the most desirable content — especially professional sports, which migrated early to cable-only formats — was limited to the most expensive subscription tiers. The cost of these top tiers has risen at two to three times the rate of inflation ever since, joining cable with education and health care as the key drivers of escalating household budgets.

Sports Über Alles

Of course, just because cable can carry a lot of channels doesn't mean it has to. The driving force behind this tiered-bundle model is the cable companies' need to cover the costs of broadcast rights for sports and other premium content. A cost breakdown of the typical top cable tier shows that the bulk of your monthly subscription fee goes to broadcast rights for a small number of channels — usually four to five.

The main culprit is sports. Every U.S. league makes millions or billions of dollars from the content networks that want to broadcast their sports. Those networks in turn reap money from cable networks, who recoup it from you via the bundle model, whether you want sports or not. Anyone who wants just a few special channels has to pay for the whole bundle regardless, keeping the money flowing up to the leagues.

One reason for this is that the content cable companies buy is also sold in bundle form. ESPN, for example, is owned by Disney, which will only sell ESPN to a cable network if it buys a range of other Disney channels as well. Each of those channels attracts a per-subscriber fee paid by the cable network, which then passes it on to subscribers whether we watch them or not.

Merging Content and Distribution

Starting with Comcast's acquisition of NBC in 2009, cable companies have rapidly merged with content producers — the people who make movies and TV shows. Cable companies realized that they might as well be the ones receiving the money they were paying for content broadcast rights, so they started acquiring the companies that produced it. In that way, they could increase their own profits — notably, by refusing to allow their now-proprietary content to be shown on competing cable networks — creating a de facto monopoly pricing situation.

Cable networks now commonly require small content programmers to give up much of their companies' equity stock just to get carried at all. As one CEO explained: "Cable and satellite TV companies want to own you before they put you on television." Cable networks are known to blackball any programmer who resists this — something illegal under federal communications and anti-trust laws, but largely unenforced.

Oligopoly

The third factor behind high and rising cable prices is regional monopolies and national industry consolidation. Many Americans rely on a single provider in their neighborhood, who can dictate prices at will. That's because most cable operators received exclusive franchises from local authorities when the cable network infrastructure was first being built out in the 1980s — using public utility rights-of-way — otherwise they wouldn't have laid the cables.

For example, in my neighborhood, Comcast was the only option for years, until AT&T figured out how to deliver cable via the existing telephone infrastructure it already owned. They're my only two choices now.

Nationally, the U.S. cable television industry is an unmistakable oligopoly, with the top four companies serving over 60% of the market. Coupled with limited regional options, this allows cable companies to jack up prices and neglect service quality at will.

Getting You Coming and Going

Finally, cable TV distributors derive extra "rent" from leasing set-top boxes to consumers. These boxes are often needed for on-demand and high-definition offerings and frequently include DVR capabilities. The cable networks dominate the market for these boxes and deliberately make it difficult for consumers to use independent boxes. As a result, the set-top box is not subject to competition or innovation (many rely on old technology); nevertheless, cable companies can and do charge high monthly prices for them.

The Specter of the Internet

The bottom line is that the average American household pays several hundred dollars a month for hundreds of cable channels … but only watches 16 of them regularly. The price of these cable packages continues to rise at more than the inflation rate, contributing to monopoly profits at our expense.

Most people instinctively react to this situation with the reasonable proposal that we should be able to buy cable channels á-la-carte, picking only those we actually watch. Surely, if we can put a man on the moon, we can pick and choose what to watch and when, paying as we go?

Indeed, there is absolutely no technological obstacle to á-la-carte television. The problem is that the cable companies rely on the current distorted market structure to extract economic rent from the U.S. consumer.

Internet streaming is the key to fighting back against this rip-off. It is considered such a threat that contracts between content producers (like ESPN) and cable networks — which are often as long as seven years — limit what the producer can make available online on its own internet streaming service. And, particularly, on third-party services such as Netflix or Apple TV. For example, ESPN still doesn't allow most live sports to be broadcast on its own streaming service, WatchESPN.

That's done specifically to ensure that streaming distributors can't compete with cable networks, so we have to keep paying excess costs for inferior products. It's market manipulation plain and simple, really.

But the cable companies aren't stupid, and they know they need to cover their flanks. So they've used those massive excess profits (rents) to buy up the broadband internet networks so that we need to watch streaming TV and ditch cable.

Consequently, nowadays most folks get their internet and cable from the same company — AT&T, Verizon, Comcast, Charter or Time Warner. That gives the cable companies even more market-distorting leverage over content producers ... and viewers like you and me. Here's how they use it:

- TV everywhere — In the late 2000s, the cable networks and the big content providers secretly colluded to create an internet-based streaming ecosystem called "TV Everywhere." The idea was to allow people to receive some streaming content — like hit cable series — but only if they already had a valid cable subscription.

  For example, there is a nice Cartoon Network "app" available for the iPhone, but you can use it only if you enter your subscription details to one of the major cable companies that carries Cartoon Network. In this way, the cable industry hoped to satisfy the demand for á-la-carte streaming without giving up any profits. They assumed what we want is the convenience to watch TV anywhere — but what we really want is the freedom to buy only what we want to watch.

- Network neutrality violations — In mafia-like fashion, cable/broadband companies like Comcast have tried to force internet-based distributors like Netflix to pay "protection money" to prevent their streams from being "throttled" or slowed down on their internet networks, making it hard to watch them online. By contrast, Comcast goes out of its way to ensure that content that it owns, like NBC shows, streams beautifully. Although the Federal Communications Commission outlawed this in 2015, it still persists in hard-to-detect forms.

- Content lockout — Cable networks that own content (such as Comcast's NBC titles) refuse to license that content to streaming TV services like Netflix, Hulu or Apple TV, forcing consumers to subscribe to Comcast cable to get it.

- Targeted cap-and-metered pricing — Recently I got a notice from AT&T, my current internet provider, saying that in May my internet data would be capped at 600 MB a month, after which I'd have to pay $25 for blocks of 50 MB. I ditched Comcast last year because they were doing the same thing (at a 300 MB cap). This lead to internet bills of $200 or more a month because I use streaming services instead of cable. There is no technological reason for them to do this, as they typically claim. Instead, they do it purely to compensate for the loss of cable subscribers to streaming services and to make returning to cable look more attractive.

An Epidemic of "Cord Cutting"

In these ways — despite the absence of technological barriers and the rapid spread of high-speed broadband internet — the cable cabal has basically blocked the natural progression to á-la-carte content in the U.S. That's why we have slower and costlier internet service and higher TV prices than any other developed country.

But 2013 turned out to be a historic inflection point: The first full year the cable industry lost subscribers. The losses widened in 2014 and rapidly grew even faster in 2015. Cable TV viewing has been dropping at around 10% a quarter, a plunge that has advertisers terrified. In the second quarter of 2015, for example, cable networks suffered their worst-ever quarterly subscriber declines, collectively shedding more than 600,000 accounts. Then in 2016, there were a reported 1.4 million fewer cable subscribers from the year prior.

Not only is the number of cable subscribers falling, but the customers who remain are buying much slimmer bundles. One result was that ESPN, the top dog of cable, reached fewer homes by the end of 2014 than it did in 2010. Nielsen announced in 2016 that ESPN had its worst reported month in its history, losing over 620,000 cable subscribers, which also meant a drop in revenue of over $52 million. Overall, the number of pay TV households is projected to decline, slowly but consistently. For example, the Statistic Brain Research Institute reported the total number of cable subscribers in 2010 to be 44,500,000, and in 2016, 34,340,000.

The driving force behind this change is "cord cutting" — the rapid uptake of the sort of streaming device and online content-delivery services. Pew Research Center's Home Broadband 2015 study found that 24% of all American adults do not subscribe to a cable TV service. Of those, 15% have become cord cutters in recent years, while

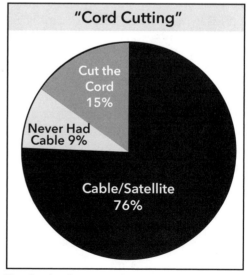

9% never had cable at all. The high cost of cable TV packages was cited by 74% of the cord cutters as the reason for dropping service. Two-thirds of those who don't subscribe to cable cited

alternate sources of streaming content as the reason for not having a traditional cable service. And 45% said they had reduced their cable or satellite TV service because they could get some desired content via streaming.

This was enough motivation for the content providers finally to take the plunge and start experimenting with streaming-only options, over the strenuous objections of the cable giants.

How I Fight Back

My household canceled its last cable subscription three years ago. At the time I was paying almost $200 a month for cable. Now I pay around $45 … and could be paying even less. And if anything, our viewing options have expanded rather than contracted … and we have vastly more control over what and when we watch.

My weapon of choice in the fight against the great cable rip-off is a little box that sits next to the TV called a Roku. (We actually have three — one in the living room, one for my daughter's room and one for the basement.) The Roku 3 box we use costs about $100, but they can be had for less on special or used on EBay, while the Roku Streaming Stick, which does the same thing, is only $45. There is no subscription charge — you just buy the Roku of your choice.

The Roku connects to our broadband internet by wireless or Ethernet cable. Once it's fired up, there's a menu of streaming "channels" to choose from. Most are free, and those that aren't are dramatically lower in price than a cable package, as you'll see shortly. We load and unload specific channels as needed — for example, during cricket season, we watch our South African national team via a special channel that we unload during the rest of the year. The same is true of many other specialized channels.

Here's the core of our Roku channel lineup:

- **Movies and TV shows** — The popular Netflix channel gives us unlimited access to tens of thousands of titles, with monthly plans that go from $7.99 for Basic to $13.99 for Premium. It also has a number of its own series, such as the popular hits "House of Cards," "Orange Is the New Black," and "Stranger Things."

Then there's Amazon Instant Video, part of Amazon Prime, which costs as low as $8.99 a month for Prime Video only, or just $12.99 a month ($119 a year) for the additional Prime perks, including two-day shipping and unlimited music streaming, photo storage, and reading. This gives us access to a large variety of video material that's "free," i.e., covered by the Prime membership. Other titles are available to buy or rent on an on-demand basis, costing anywhere from 99 cents to several dollars per title. We typically pay $4.99 for the standard definition version of a movie that has just been in theatres. After a few months, the price of such films drops to $2.99 or $1.99. High definition is also available, usually for $1 more per title. Amazon Prime added the ability to stream versions of popular cable channels, such as Starz, Showtime, and HBO, with free trials or monthly fees ranging from $8.99, $10.99 and $14.99, respectively.

Finally, my wife subscribes to the CBS All Access channel ($5.99 a month), which carries her favorite soap opera.

- **News** — All the major American news networks, including CNN and PBS, have Roku channels that provide both a live feed and a menu of specific stories viewable on demand. The live feed isn't always the same as what you'd see on cable, but it's pretty close. Some of the networks display adverts between news segments, just like a broadcast signal, but they are much shorter and less obtrusive. Local news channels are available on Roku for every major and medium-sized city in the U.S. I also subscribe to a range of alternative news networks — the list of available channels grows every day.

- **Sports** — Here's where my household is atypical. Since we're South African-Americans, we follow cricket, rugby and soccer, mainly. We can get those sports either via a special channel (Willow TV) or as part of a free ESPN or Fox Sports Roku channel. We pay for the cricket channel, which has live broadcasts, but for rugby and soccer we often watch free replays the next day.

On the other hand, if we were into American sports, we could simply subscribe to Sling TV for $25 a month, which would give us ESPN, ESPN 2, NBA basketball and a number of entertainment channels. In addition, we might add MLB.TV for our favorite baseball team ($50/year) and NFL Game Pass ($100/year). Both are also available month-by month. The NHL GameCenter platform and Major League Soccer's MLS Live provide similar access for those sports. College sports channels are also available at similar prices for games that aren't already on ESPN.

Note, however, that this may not be enough if you're a diehard. The old-fashioned, network-oriented licensing and marketing rules usually entail a blackout of local team games, forcing you either to watch them on local network TV affiliates, or to watch them later on replay.

History Repeating: Broadband Consolidation

The top high-speed internet access providers include cable companies AT&T, Comcast, Verizon, Time Warner, Cox and others. These companies charge you twice — once for internet access and once for a cable TV subscription.

Most analysts predict that as customers desert cable TV packages for internet-based streaming services, the telecom giants will try to charge more for internet, wiping out some or all of the cable savings. Indeed, the raw economics of internet delivery favor the cable companies. Internet service is much cheaper to offer than TV, so having customers shift the balance of their bills to data instead of TV is pure profit for the industry. It costs broadband providers virtually nothing if you use more data, so the overage charges they are starting to apply for the higher data usage arising from streaming cord cutters is essentially easy money for them.

That's why it's important to pay attention to the debates about competition in the broadband market and issues like net neutrality. The cable/internet giants are lobbying furiously for special favors from national and local politicians to protect their extraction of excess profits from the rest of us.

For example, some states have passed laws that make it difficult or impossible for municipalities to invest in low-cost broadband networks for their residents. They have also erected barriers that make it hard for newer businesses to string fiber-optic cable on utility poles or below ground in order to compete with established cable and phone companies.

The Digital Antenna Hack

But there's a way around that, which also gives you access to local broadcast stations in real-time — the digital antenna or HD antenna. Local affiliates of commercial broadcast networks like CBS, NBC, ABC and Fox still broadcast free-to-air the way they always have, except that now the signal is digital. With a digital antenna, you can ditch cable but still get real-time broadcast networks for free. Modern HD antennas don't have to go on the roof — they're simple affairs you set up next to the TV. (Outdoor antennas remain a viable option.) You'll have to play with the antenna position to maximize reception, just like fiddling with rabbit ear antennas in the 1970s.

Before you do this, make sure you have over-the-air HD as an option where you live. Visit AntennaWeb (www.antennaweb. org) or TV Fool (http://www.tvfool.com) for a listing of the stations broadcasting near you and the sort of antenna you might need to pick them up. Top-rated HD indoor antennas include the Winegard FL5500A FlatWave Amplified Razor Thin HD Indoor Antenna and Mohu Leaf 50 Amplified Indoor HD Antenna, both in the $50 to $60 range.

Your Options for Low-Cost Streaming

There are a lot of ways to watch streaming TV across the internet like I do. For these services, a five megabyte per second (Mbps) broadband internet connection is generally fine, although high-definition streams may require a bit more.

Your viewing options include your smartphone, tablet, computer and, of course, your TV. On your computer, just visit a streaming service's website to view them — or connect your laptop to your TV using a monitor output, as I sometimes do for special events that are only on the internet.

An increasingly popular option is to use "smart" TVs, which have built-in streaming software like Roku and connect to the internet. I was in Best Buy recently and saw excellent 52" models on sale for under $450.

If you don't have a smart TV, there are many streaming hub options like the Roku I use with an eight-year-old flat screen. They include game consoles such as the Xbox 360, Xbox One, PlayStation 3, PlayStation 4 and Nintendo Wii. Several Blu-ray players also have streaming hub apps.

Dedicated streaming devices like my Roku have two main forms: a thumb-drive sized unit that plugs into the HDMI port on the TV or a separate box the size of a portable CD player. Excellent small "stick" streaming devices include the Google Chromecast ($35), Roku Streaming Stick ($50) or the Amazon Fire TV Stick ($40). Larger units like my Roku 3 that give slightly better performance and on-board memory storage include the Amazon Fire TV and the Apple TV, and the newer Roku 4K.

Every single one of these products supports the holy "trinity" of cord cutter video-streaming apps: Netflix, Hulu and Amazon Prime Instant Video. If you've got a specific service you want to watch, however, you need to do some research. Not every streaming devices or game console gives access to every streaming service. For example, PlayStation 4 users who have Comcast cable have found that the company blocks them from using the HBO GO app that was recently released for that console.

What's You'll Save

Here's the list of apps that would give you almost complete programming coverage — at least of primetime TV across networks and cable channels. Many of them offer a free month trial, too.

From this you can do a quick calculation against your current cable bill. Remember that you'll need to keep internet service, so be sure to deduct that from your current billing if you get bundled service to arrive at your cable-only cost.

In any case, our household has saved a substantial amount of money each month. Now, we don't subscribe to all the streaming services — I don't have Hulu, HBO Now or Sling TV. But everyone in my household is perfectly happy with what we get. We do purchase on-demand movies and TV shows two to three times a week, which probably adds another $40 to our monthly outlay — but remember, these are things we choose to watch, and when to watch them. We don't need to set up a recording — just click and view on demand.

Service	Monthly	Yearly
Netflix "Standard"	$10.99	$131.88
Hulu	$7.99	$95.88
Amazon Prime	$12.99	$119.00
Sling TV ("Orange" or "Blue")	$25.00	$300.00
HBO Now	$14.99	$179.88
CBS All Access	$5.99	$71.88
TOTAL	$77.95	$898.52

Is Cord Cutting for You?

The decision to "cut the cord" as I've done depends on how you balance the various factors. To help you do that, here's a summary of the pros and cons:

Pros −

- **Savings:** If you're like me, you'll definitely save money. Theoretically, you could pay almost as much as you do for cable if you subscribe to a lot of streaming services. I did initially try a number of the other streaming services that I don't use, but just found that I didn't watch enough on them to justify the cost. When the dust settled down, I was saving almost $150 a month.

- **Flexibility and convenience:** A big overlooked factor with cord cutting is that nearly everything becomes on demand. You don't have to watch when the show is on — you watch when you want to do so.

  You don't have to watch the movie HBO is showing to-night — you pick one yourself. In some cases — such as AMC's "The Walking Dead", a big hit in my household — we watch it the day after it shows on cable, which doesn't bother us one bit. We just ignore the reviews until we've seen it.

- **No contracts:** All of the streaming services we use except Amazon Instant Video are on a month-to-month basis, and I can cancel or suspend them at any time with no con-sequence. Some U.S. sports packages require an annual payment, but most allow you to go month-to-month as well. Compare that to the silly contracts and conciliation rules cable companies impose on you!

- **Fewer things to go wrong:** Streaming video requires only internet, a streaming device and a TV or monitor. At its simplest, all you need is your computer. That's a great deal less complicated than the cables and set-top boxes required by cable setups. When we had Comcast cable, we had service outages nearly every month. We've never once had a problem with our streaming setup.

Cons −

- **Lost content:** The biggest con is the loss of some chan-nels, especially live news and major sports. Some popular shows are only available after a delay, as I noted above, and this may matter to you. But honestly, considering the abysmal quality of most U.S. cable news, is that such a big deal? In any case, streaming offers are expanding rapidly, and I anticipate that content restrictions will fade just as fast.

- **Vulnerability to abuse of internet monopoly:** As I noted in the box earlier, the cable giants are trying to combat cord cutting by chiseling us on the broadband internet side. Right now, for example, if I had a Comcast internet package, my typical streaming usage would incur significant additional broadband overage fees every month, which would cancel out the advantage of dropping cable. Fortunately, I have alternatives — Google Fiber is on its way to my town — so this isn't an issue. But it may be for you. I do predict, however, that the cable companies will ultimately lose the fight to extract excess profits via abuse of broadband markets, particularly with Google and Apple moving rapidly to enter the broadband market directly.

Conclusion

There's nothing stopping you from trying out cord cutting right now. Just get a streaming box or stick and check it out, and keep your cable until you're ready to decide. Even if you decide to stick with cable, it'll still come in handy — after all, you can take it with you when you travel in the U.S. and view Netflix and so on anywhere you can get a suitable internet connection.

Give it a try — I promise you won't regret it. And remember … it's not just about the money … it's about what's right for all of us.

INCOME SECRET NO. 37:

Separate Your Landline
Long-Distance Phone Carrier

The majority of households today subscribe to "bundle" services from multi telecommunication providers, which include phone, cable and internet. When considering a "bundle," you should ask yourself, "does bundling really save me money?"

Providers have built up — through their ads and sales strategies — the idea that you are better off to subscribe to their bundle deals. But having all the components ordered together may not be saving you money, especially if you don't need all of them. Many of us also don't pay close attention to what we are paying for and just pay the bill each month. If you go over your bill in detail, you may find that you are being deceived into believing you are getting a "deal."

When considering bundle options, if you find yourself needing to keep a landline in your home, instead of bundling phone services, consider separating them. There are several long-distance phone carriers that charge relatively cheaper rates for long distance phone calls.

Here's how it works: These carriers charge about three cents or four cents per minute with six-second billing increments. There are no minimums nor monthly fees.

If you were to call someone out of state and talk for over an hour, your bill could be as low as $5 or $6, including taxes and fees, for the month.

And if you do not talk to anyone in a month, your bill is $0.

A company that can offer such savings is Pioneer Telephone. Since 1994, Pioneer states that it has helped "business and residential customers save on their phone bill. Over $1,003,206,851 in savings to date, and [they] are just getting started." For more details, visit http://www.pioneertelephone.com.

Other strategies that you can consider to lower your phone expense is to go mobile and get rid of your landline altogether. The majority of mobile plans include unlimited phone and text within the continental United States.

You can also use apps and computer-based software, such as WhatsApp and Skype. These applications allow you to phone local and international numbers at no cost.

In addition, there is the option to use a Voice over Internet Protocol (VoIP) provider, such as Vonage (https://www.vonage.com/personal). A VoIP transmits phone calls using a digital connection.

The bottom line is you can save yourself money each month by examining how you utilize your phone and what you use it for. Cut out what you don't need and take advantage of all the great options that cost close to nothing, if nothing at all.

INCOME SECRET NO. 38:

Save up to $45 Per Month by Replacing Furnace and Air Filters Regularly

Sooner or later, homeowners and small-business owners need to clean or replace their furnace and air filters. However, if you want to save money on your energy costs, sooner is much better than later.

Regularly replacing filters — every 30 to 90 days depending on the make and model of the filter — allows air to flow easily without overtaxing the HVAC blower motor. Not only does less stress on the equipment extend the life of your heating and cooling system, it can also save you up to $45 per month.

According to FilterSnap.com website:

The Department of Energy states that replacing a dirty filter with a clean one can reduce energy consumption by as much as 15%. Combine that with the knowledge that your HVAC is responsible for approximately half your energy bill, and you're looking at savings of 7.5% every month.

So, if your average electric bill is $100 per month, you could save approximately $7.50 by changing your filter regularly (or, you are already saving that much if you change them regularly). Over three months, that's $22.50. That said, if your energy bill is only $100 per month, good on you.

If your bill is closer to the $200 range — and it can likely creep up there when the furnace or A/C is working daily to heat or cool your house — you're looking at savings of up to $45 per month.

When shopping for an air filter make sure to look at the MERV rating (minimum efficiency report value). The higher the MERV rating, the less unwanted particles, dust and debris pass through the filter. These ratings range from 1 (lowest efficiency) to 20 (highest efficiency).

- MERV ratings 1 through 4 trap pollen, dust mites, sanding dust, spray paint dust, textile and carpet fibers. This range is for minimum filtration and used mostly in residential buildings.

- MERV ratings 5 through 8 also trap mold spores, hair spray, fabric protector, cement dust and pet dander. This range is typically used in better residential or general commercial and industrial workspaces.

- MERV ratings 9 through 12 go a step further and trap humidifier dust, lead dust, auto emissions and milled flour. This rating range is typically used in superior residential buildings or better commercial buildings.

- MERV ratings 13 through 16 trap all particles ranked 1 to 12 and go the extra mile by trapping bacteria, most tobacco smoke, droplet nuclei (sneeze), most face powder and cooking oil. This rating range is typically used in superior commercial buildings and hospitals.

- MERV rating 17 through 20, the top rating tier, is typically used in pharmaceutical and electronics cleanrooms.

True, air filters cost about $10 to $20 each, but what you save in replacing them every three months more than makes up for the expense — and puts even more money in your pocket over the long run.

INCOME SECRET NO. 39:

Save Hundreds in Energy Costs Just by Switching to the Right Light Bulb

According to the U.S. Department of Energy, the average American household dedicates about 5% of its energy budget to lighting. However, according to the Environmental Protection Agency (EPA), approximately 70% of all U.S. light bulb sockets still contain inefficient light bulbs. Whereas, if Americans made the switch to Energy Star-certified LED light bulbs, they could realize savings of up to $118 million in energy costs!

That's because just one Energy Star-certified LED light bulb saves about $6 a year in electricity costs and can save anywhere from $40 to $135 over its lifetime. Which means that you can light your home for less money and cut your overall energy bills by switching to energy-efficient lighting.

Ninety percent of the energy used by traditional incandescent bulbs is given off as heat, which is an inefficient waste of energy. It's one of the reasons incandescent bulbs are no longer being manufactured and are being replaced with money-saving options such as halogen incandescent, compact fluorescent lamps (CFL), and light-emitting diodes (LED) light bulbs. It is estimated that by replacing your home's five most frequently used light fixtures with bulbs that have earned the Energy Star rating, you can save as much as $75 each year.

These newer choices in energy-efficient lighting come in the same colors and light levels as before. Although they cost more than traditional incandescent bulbs, they last far longer because they use less energy and, therefore, save you money over the long term.

In addition, you can install controls such timers and photocells that save electricity by turning lights off when not in use. Also, dimmers save electricity when used to lower light levels. In terms of outdoor lighting, CFLs or LEDs can be used in a variety of fixtures to save energy. Most bare spiral CFLs can be enclosed in fixtures that protect them from the elements. CFLs and LEDs are also available as flood lights. Many outdoor Energy Star-qualified fixtures come with features such as automatic daylight shut-off and motion sensors.

Here's a quick review of your energy-efficient alternatives:

- Halogen incandescent — This type of bulb has a capsule inside that contains gas around a filament to increase the bulb's efficiency. It's available in various shapes and colors, and can be used with dimmers. Although it meets federal minimum energy efficiency standards, there are more efficient options available.

- CFLs — These are curly versions of the long tube fluorescent lights you may already be using in your kitchen or garage. Since they use less electricity than traditional incandescent bulbs, CFLs pay for themselves in less than nine months, then save you money each month. In fact, an Energy Star-qualified CFL uses just one-fourth the energy of a traditional incandescent bulb and one-third the energy of a halogen incandescent, while providing the same amount of light and lasting 10 times longer than the traditional incandescent bulb.

- LEDs — These are a type of solid-state lighting in which semiconductors convert electricity into light. LEDs that are Energy Star-qualified use only 20% to 25% of the energy of traditional incandescent bulbs and last up to 25 times longer. Similarly, they use 25% to 30% of the energy of halogen incandescent bulbs and last eight to 25 times longer.

  LED bulbs are available as replacements for 40-, 60- and 75-watt traditional incandescent bulbs, reflector bulbs used in recessed fixtures, desk lamps, track lights, under cabinet lighting and outdoor area lights. Some are dimmable and can also be used as daylight and motion sensors. Another advantage of LEDs is that they perform well both indoors and outdoors because of their durability in cold environments, making them an excellent choice for pathway lighting, step lighting and porch lights.

INCOME SECRET NO. 40:

Save up to $20 Per Month by Tinting Your Home Windows

When looking to save on your household energy bills, don't overlook this "bright" idea: tinting your home windows.

For homes in warmer climates that have a direct eastern or western exposure to sunlight, tinting your windows with at least 28% visible light transfer (VLT) shade film can help save between $10 to $20 per month on your monthly energy bills, depending on the size of your home.

Window tinting has been an option for more than 50 years. It has become the norm for automotive application, but residential window tinting is still gradually gaining in popularity. That's because window-tinting technologies have greatly improved over the years to become a useful tool in reducing energy costs associated with heating and cooling your home.

Contrary to what some believe, you don't have to darken your windows to achieve effective heat reduction.

One option is ceramic window tint, which can block up to 90% of infrared heat without eliminating daylight.

Likewise, various solar-control films can block up to 80% of the sun's radiant heat coming through your windows. According to the International Window Film Association, that can result in a year-round savings of about 5% to 10% of your home's total energy bill — and possibly more during hot months.

Not only can residential window tinting save you money by reducing your energy bill, but it can also save you money on interior renovation. The visible light that enters your home through your windows lies on the spectrum between ultraviolet and infrared. Ultraviolet radiation can damage your furniture, while infrared radiation emits heat.

Tinted windows, however, can block 99% of UVA and UVB rays, thus slowing the deterioration and fading of drapes, carpet and furniture. It can also protect you and your family from harmful UV rays.

Residential window tinting can transform your home into a safer, more comfortable environment while saving you a bundle in energy costs over the long term. For more information about home window tinting, visit www.iwfa.com.

INCOME SECRET NO. 41:

Save up to 30% on Your Heating and Cooling Bills With This 1 Simple Trick

According to the U.S. Department of Energy, heating and cooling account for about 48% of the energy use in a typical U.S. home, making it the largest energy expense for most homes.

That being the case, you stand to save a substantial amount of your income by conserving energy in your home wherever you can.

One of the best ways to do that is by installing a programmable thermostat to regulate your home's temperature — whether you live in a warm or cold climate.

According to the U.S. Department of Energy, a programmable thermostat can help you save as much as 10% a year on heating and cooling by turning thermostats down 7 to 10 degrees for eight hours per day from its usual setting. In all, when used correctly, these thermostats can save 10% to 30% on cooling and heating bills.

If you're unsure how high or low to set your thermostat in the summer and winter, follow these industry recommendations:

- **During the summer** — Generally speaking, our bodies are most comfortable indoors when the air is within a degree or two of 75 degrees Fahrenheit during hot summer months. However, this temperature setting isn't necessary when your home is unoccupied. So, if you're out of the house for long periods during the day — at work or doing errands — set the temperature several degrees higher. Setting the temperature a few degrees higher during the cooler night before bedtime is also an energy-saving practice worth considering. Following this routine for eight-hour intervals will greatly reduce your cooling cost. Just don't overdo it because it will make it that much harder for your A/C unit to reach your comfort level if the air temperature gets too warm.

- **During the winter** — Your furnace or heating unit will keep you comfortably warm during colder months if your thermostat is set at 68 degrees Fahrenheit. And, just like in the summer, lowering your thermostat a few degrees at eight-hour intervals when you aren't home or snug in your bed will save money on your heating bills. Plus, during milder winter days — or if you have a fireplace — you may not have to use your furnace or heating unit at all.

- **When you're away from home** — Do not shut your cooling or heating system off completely if you go on vacation or take a weekend getaway. That will only lead to high humidity levels that spawn mold growth during hot summers since your home's interior temperature will soar uncontrollably and fresh air won't circulate. Likewise, allowing your house to drastically cool down while you're away during frigid winter months will make your system work much harder to warm up your home when you return. Instead, set your thermostat at a constant temperature that's several degrees higher than normal during summer trips, and several degrees lower during winter getaways. Plus, having your outdoor condensing unit running occasionally will make it appear that someone is home, providing a measure of security.

For a detailed energy assessment of your home that includes money-saving recommendations for thermostat use, contact your local utility.

INCOME SECRET NO. 42:

Save Energy and Money by Setting Your Ceiling Fans to a Low Speed

We all know that air conditioning can be a costly necessity in hot weather, but it also can be an expensive luxury all year round when there's an effective and thriftier climate control alternative — ceiling fans.

While a typical central air conditioning unit uses 3,500 watts of energy when in use, the average ceiling fan uses a mere 60 watts — even at a high speed. That, according to thesimpledollar.com, means that if running your ceiling fan all day long allows you to reduce your AC usage — even for just 30 minutes per day — you could save a significant amount of money over time.

And if you follow these energy-efficient tips, who knows how much you might be able to save in energy costs while staying comfortable in your home:

- **Adjust the direction of your ceiling fan so the air blows down in summer.** Your fan should have a "clockwise" and "counterclockwise" setting. Each of these settings is appropriate for a different season. During the summer, you should have your ceiling running on high in a counterclockwise direction to force the air down and cool the room.

- **Run the fan on low in the other direction in the winter.** In colder winter months, flip the little switch or push the button near the base of your fan so that it turns clockwise. This will pull air up in the center of the room and push it down again along the outer edges. What this does is force warm air and cool to mingle, keeping the room at a steadier temperature. It prevents heat from rising and building at the top and cool air from settling near the floor, so your furnace or heating system doesn't have to work so hard to keep your home warm. If you stand near a wall in the room, you should feel a gentle, warm breeze.

- **Set your thermostat higher in the summer.** Raise the temperature by a few degrees if you are planning on running your ceiling fans constantly on a hot day. While your ceiling fan doesn't directly cool the air, it does help circulate the cool air better, creating a breeze effect that can make the room feel cooler than it really is.

- **Be sure to turn off your ceiling fans when you leave home.** This can save your money as well. There's no sense in keeping your home quite as cool or warm as normal when you aren't there. If you have a programmable thermostat, you can set your air conditioning unit to turn off and on based on the time when you'll be home.

It makes basic economic sense; who needs the high cost of overused air conditioning when low-cost ceiling fans can keep you cool or warm all year long?

INCOME SECRET NO. 43:

Get Paid to Clear Out Your Clutter

Over the course of just one year, it can be surprising to see how many items we can accumulate. We pick up things to make our life easier or mementos from a trip or new experience. These wonderful items exist in almost every nook and cranny in our own homes.

Now is an excellent time to go through all of your belongings, and decide what should be kept and what should be donated or discarded and then get PAID.

And nowadays, you don't have to rely on simply dropping off to a donation center, or dump, or even having those all-day garage sales.

In fact, if you have a smart phone or access to the internet, getting rid of unwanted things is easy. As the old adage says, someone's junk is someone else's treasure.

Here are some of the best free apps, to help you clean the clutter and even make some money:

- OfferUp — This app and site allows you to browse local items, by image with thousands of new postings every day, and communicate with sellers entirely through their in-app messaging. Simply take a photo, post the description and price and get ready to take the best offer. People are selling everything from cars to grills to shoes to ocean kayaks.

- LetGo — This is another free app and website where you can sell (and buy) pre-owned stuff. It is very similar to OfferUp, but better organized by categories.

Now, for some of us, having a garage sale is an overwhelming amount of work, and in some communities, it is prohibited. So, another route you can take is donating the items to charity.

Although there are several national and local agencies that will gladly take your donations, it's always best to call first to make sure they are accepting donations and in what form.

And, don't forget, donations are tax deductible! Be sure to keep your receipts for tax purposes.

Recently, I came across a great app that will let you track and value your non-cash charitable donations. The app iDonate-dIt is dedicated to helping you get the most value possible from your charitable donation. This app is available on the Apple App Store.

When you're done, you'll have more room in your home and money in your pocket.

INCOME SECRET NO. 44:

Win up to $10,000 Playing Digital Scratch-Off Lotteries Each Day ... for Free

Scratch-off lottery tickets are fun and — if you're really, really lucky — you can win anywhere from a few bucks to thousands of dollars.

The only problem is that these tickets cost you money. And with astronomical odds of winning a big prize against you, it's one of the worst "investments" you could make.

If only you could play for free and win some cash every now and then.

Actually, you can with the Lucktastic app that lets you play digital scratch-off lotteries every day for free. It's a fun way to win cash and prizes worth up to $10,000.

To start playing and winning, all you have to do is download the Lucktastic app at the iTunes App Store or Google Play Store. Follow the instructions on opening an account and you're good to go.

To win any scratch card, you need to match three of the winning symbols displayed on that digit card. If you win a cash prize, you'll receive a notification within the app congratulating you, and your winnings will appear in your account balance.

Yeah, but what about the odds?

For instance, scratch cards depend on the number of people playing the cards. For contests, the odds of winning depend on the number of entries received. But all entries have the same chance of winning, and the winner won't be announced until he or she has confirmed their information.

As for that $10,000 scratch card, you have to play a total of 150 scratch cards to unlock it, but all scratch cards count toward that goal. Once you've unlocked the $10,000 card, it stays unlocked and you can check your progress at any time on your personal Lucktastic dashboard.

Redeeming Lucktastic Instant Rewards is easy.

Once you have accumulated enough tokens, you simply go to the Instant Rewards section, tap the four-leaf clover icon in the top left corner of your app, select Instant Rewards, and choose the Instant Reward you want to claim. You'll be prompted to verify your account and enter your phone number, and then you'll receive a text message with a six-digit code to confirm your identity. From there, you'll receive an email and/or SMS message with a link to your electronic gift card.

To date, Lucktastic has awarded over $3 million in prizes and rewards to more than a million players. You could be next. It costs nothing to download the app and play, yet you could come away a winner.

For more detailed information about Lucktastic, including how to get started earning rewards, visit https://lucktastic.com/faq.

INCOME SECRET NO. 45:

Get Automatic Refunds With This Little-Known Email App

How often have you purchased an item on sale or for the full retail price only to discover shortly thereafter that the price has been reduced even more? It's a frustrating feeling and an inconvenience if it means having to return the item for a better deal.

Or maybe you aren't even aware that the price has gone down and that you could have acquired the item for less than you paid.

As a consumer, you rarely have the time, resources or presence of mind to backtrack and check for price drop, much less call or email the retailer to get your refund.

That's where Paribus can save you hundreds, if not thousands of dollars, per year.

The company has an app that does the legwork for you. It tracks customer and price adjustment policies at popular online merchants. When it sees a potential savings or refund opportunity based on your purchase history, it contacts the merchant on your behalf to help get you the refund.

The Paribus app is 100% free and available at the iTunes App Store.

Here's how it works:

You download the app and register with Paribus, authorizing it to act as your agent. Using the same advanced data structures and algorithms that retailers use to fix prices, Paribus collects your refunds in part by scanning your emails for receipts from your recent purchases. It identifies your receipt, evaluates the data and imports it into its database, focusing on the price at which you purchased the item. Your refund period generally lasts for about two weeks. During that time, Paribus monitors the cost of the product and submits a refund request on your behalf if the price drops.

Among the online merchants on Paribus' radar are:

Amazon	Banana Republic	Costco
Bloomingdale's	Gap	Home Depot
Macy's	Old Navy	Sears
Staples	Walmart	Crate & Barrel
Target	Kohl's	Bed Bath & Beyond
J. Crew	Office Depot	Anthropologie
Zappos	Neiman Marcus	L.L. Bean
Nordstrom	Saks Fifth Avenue	Wayfair

The Paribus homepage shows examples of refunds that fetch you anywhere from at least $3 to over $300, depending on the item you purchased and the price drop Paribus finds.

Not only does the Paribus app offer price protection by watching for price drops at online retailers with price adjustment policies, but it streamlines the claim process to make it easier for you to promptly get your money back.

Also, Paribus offers delivery monitoring, tracking your shipments from select online retailers to see if you are owed money for late deliveries.

For more information about the Paribus app and how it can help save you a bundle in refunds, visit the company's website at https://paribus.co.

PASSION TO PROFITS

Adding to your income doesn't mean that you need to take on a typical nine-to-five job. Resourceful people have come up with exciting and creative sources of income in the new "gig economy." This is an opportunity to dedicate a little of your free time and possibly some skills that you've learned over years to raking in some extra cash. Learn how you can earn some extra money with the photos you took on your last vacation. Turn your favorite hobby into an easy source of cash. You can even get paid doing routine activities such as watching TV. Turn your passion into profit.

INCOME SECRET NO. 46:

Get Paid to Do Routine Activities

In a perfect world, they'd pay you to watch TV. You'd get a bonus for paying your bills each month, and you'd collect $100 or more for stopping by your hair salon or barber shop.

Well, welcome to that perfect world.

You can do all of those things. And here's how...

First of all, there are numerous companies that will pay you to watch videos and TV shows. For example, Netflix, the most popular subscription video streaming service on the planet, periodically hires "taggers" — or editorial analysts, if you want to get technical about it. These are folks who watch Netflix's programming and enter relevant metadata (words or phrases that describe the content) into the company's database to make it easier to search and categorize and also to provide accurate recommendations to fellow subscribers.

According to MoneyPantry.com, Netflix taggers watch approximately ten to twenty hours of programming per week, earning on average $300 per week. These positions are posted on the Netflix job board (https://jobs.netflix.com) and are perfect if you like to binge-watch movies, TV series and special programming.

Of course, there are only a limited number of positions available at Netflix, and the competition for them is fierce. But they're not the only game in town. There are many other pay-to-watch TV services.

One of them is Marketforce Information, which has a "Certified Field Associate" program (https://www.certifiedfieldassociate. com) that pays you $10 to $20 per hour to watch Netflix or to be a Theater Checker, visiting movie theaters on the weekends and — among other things — collecting box office information or recording all trailers on all screens prior to the assigned feature.

And then there's Swagbucks (https://www.swagbucks.com), where you can earn money for watching a variety of themed videos ranging from world news to sports and entertainment. When you're ready to be paid, you can redeem your bucks for gift cards or PayPal cash.

Inbox Dollars (https://www.inboxdollars.com) also allows you to make money watching short videos on a daily basis. You get paid with cash and earn your first $5 just for signing up.

Not interested in spending a lot of time at the movies or in front of the tube? Here's another option: Download the MoneyLion app. It offers rewards — including gift cards to restaurants such as Chili's, Romano's Macaroni Grill, Maggiano's and On The Border, and to AMC Theaters — for staying on top of your finances.

That's right — you earn rewards by:

- Signing up for a free MoneyLion account (1,400 points).
- Downloading the mobile app (100 points).
- Connecting a bank account to track spending (500 points).
- Sign up for free credit monitoring (250 points).
- Make bill payments on time (50 points).
- Get a loan (200 points).
- More rewards with MoneyLion Plus Cashback bonuses — $1 every day just for logging into the MoneyLion app (exclusive to MoneyLion Plus members).

For more information or to join, visit www.MoneyLion.comrewards.

Now, while discussing ways to earn rewards for doing what otherwise are daily routines, here is a way to get cash back.

Ebates is a cash back and discount website that helps its members earn when spending. What does that mean for you? All you have to do it become a member — free of charge — and begin your online shopping at www.ebates.com. From there, you'll find over 2,500 of the biggest stores and boutiques, including Amazon, Macy's, Kohl's, Zulily, Home Depot, even Travelocity. From that, you can earn as much as 10% cash back.

Simple search for the store you want, sign in, and shop. From that, you get a check in the mail or can be paid through a PayPal payment. It's that simple! Seemingly almost too good to be true. Plus, you can get a $10 bonus just for signing up. This is the ultimate easy way to make money for doing what you would be doing anyway.

And finally, this hair-raising opportunity…

Every time you go for a haircut, your locks end up on the salon or barbershop floor, where they usually get swept up and disposed of. Instead, you can sell your hair for anywhere from $100 to $4,000!

As long as you have hair that is at least six inches long, there are buyers from around the world — often wig manufacturers — who'll pay good money for those precious strands. All you need to do is go to Hairsellon.com, register for a free account, post an ad and wait for the offers to come pouring in.

And the great thing about hair is that it'll grow back, so you can make this an ongoing, profitable side hustle.

For more information, visit www.hairsellon.com.

INCOME SECRET NO. 47:

Earn Thousands Per Year Writing About Your Favorite Hobby Online

Do you have a favorite hobby? Perhaps it's collecting memorabilia, restoring vintage cars, photography, crafting … the list goes on and on.

Chances are, many other people share your interest and would like to learn more about it and/or profit from this knowledge. So why not start a blog and write about it on a regular basis?

How exactly do you make money from blogging? By being more than just a writer, but also an entrepreneur running a small business and using your blog as a lead generator for products and services.

Blogging can earn you money in several ways … from simple Google AdSense revenue to affiliate sales.

With AdSense (https://www.google.com/adsense), you place Google ads on your website. When a visitor clicks on it, Google pays you 68% of what the advertiser pays them.

Affiliate sales are a business model in which you endorse someone else's products or services in exchange for a commission — typically 50% or more.

How much you make by blogging depends on the quality of your blog, how long it's been online and how much traffic is directed to your site.

A survey of 1,500 ProBlogger readers found the majority made only about $1,278, but 9% made between $1,000 and $10,000 per month and 4% made over $10,000 per month.

So, how do you become a part of the 13%? The process, according to ProBlogger, involves:

- **Setting up your blog.** First, you choose a topic for your blog (for example, health, marketing or gardening) and focus on that one topic. Next, you pick a relevant domain name and purchase it. Then find an affordable web host, install WordPress and upload a good-looking template so your blog looks professional.

- **Creating useful content.** To make your blog worth reading, you'll need to research keywords your audience is typing into search engines. You'll find these using keyword tools such as SEMrush, Ahrefs and the Google Keyword Planner. Also, research the kind of content shared on social media. This can be done by running blogs on the same topic as yours through BuzzSumo, which analyzes what content performs best.

- **Converting visitors to email subscribers.** How much money you make as a blogger will depend on how many recurring visitors you have. Ways to lure subscribers include an email marketing platform (to send mass emails), sign-up forms on the blog and a bribe to subscribe in the form of a free giveaway.

- **Building engagement with readers.** Before sending readers links to your sales pages, build their trust by delivering content that provides them with great value for free. When they realize your advice actually works, they'll not only trust you but also be more likely to purchasing the products or services you have to offer.

- **Making money from a variety of income streams by selling products or services your audience wants.** These can include:

  o Education such as coaching, courses, books, e-books and seminars.

  o Services such as financial, programming, design, copywriting and marketing.

  o Digital goods such as templates, music, software, photography and games.

  o Physical goods such as art, electronics, clothing, supplements and food.

There are many sites devoted to showing you how to build a successful blog. These include: Backlinko, DigitalMarketer and Smart Passive Income. And for more tips on starting and maintaining a moneymaking blog, visit: https://smartblogger.com/make-money-blogging.

INCOME SECRET NO. 48:

Turn a Lifetime of Knowledge Into Cash

When your children were growing up, there were probably a lot of nights that you sat at the kitchen table, helping them with their math or science homework. Or maybe you were an ace at flashcards. Or maybe you helped them achieve that next reading level through nightly lessons.

While your kids might be grown and raising their own kids, that doesn't mean your nights of tutoring are over.

Only this time, you could get paid for your time in actual cash.

At Tutors.com, it costs anywhere from $25 to $100 per hour for tutoring help in the subject areas of math, economics, languages, sciences and programming. Most tutors start at around $11 per hour, but your pay rate varies based on the difficulty of the subject and can increase as you gain experience.

Some high demand areas of knowledge include:

- Calculus.
- Discrete Math.
- Physics.
- Chemistry/Organic Chemistry.
- Statistics/College Statistics.
- Finance.
- Economics.
- Accounting.
- German.
- French.
- Italian
- Nursing.

Another option is Chegg Tutors (https://www.chegg.com). The company has higher requirements for its tutors, but those tutors will be paid $20 per hour at the start.

Use your free time to help someone expand their knowledge and earn money.

INCOME SECRET NO. 49:

Spending Time With Man's Best Friend Can Increase Your Income

We love our four-legged friends. They are companions and a frequent source of amusement and love in our lives.

But vacations and emergencies that draw us away from home means we need someone reliable to care for our dog or cat.

That's where the reliable pet sitter comes in.

Pet Sitters International reported that the pet sitting industry reached $332 million in revenue at 720,000 households nationally in 2014. And it's still growing.

Pet sitting offers the pet a calm, private home rather than the noise and anxiety of a kennel environment.

And if you're an animal lover, this is an easy way to make some extra money out of your own home without a lot of effort. For pet sitting, there's no extensive training or certifications required.

On sites such as Rover (https://www.rover.com) or Care. com (https://www.care.com/pet-care), you can post a profile, which will include your rates (e.g., $25 per night or $15 to $20 per hour), your availability and photos of yourself, your family, any pets you may have and the space your animal guest will be staying in.

The director of operations for Rover.com estimates that a person who treats pet sitting as a part-time job, taking two or three dogs for two weeks out of a month will earn $1,000 per month on average.

Someone treating pet sitting as a full-time job can earn roughly $3,300 a month on average.

If you're an animal lover, that's an easy way to rake in a little extra income doing something you already enjoy.

INCOME SECRET NO. 50:

Earn $5 Every Time You Snap a Photo
With Your Mobile Phone

What are you paying per month for that rad mobile phone of yours? It does everything, right? Places calls and texts messages. Takes sharp, awesome photos.

What if I told you that you could make that phone pay for itself and then some?

Instead of snapping selfies and posting them on social media for nothing more than instant gratification, why not snap photos of other things — sunsets, landmarks, vistas, public events, gourmet foods, adorable pets, you name it — and sell those photos for $5 a shot?

That's exactly what you can do with the Foap smartphone app available on Google Play and the iTunes App Store.

With the Foap app, you can do more than just create your own portfolio and stock it with unlimited uploads. You can upload your photos straight from your phone and sell them through Foap Missions to brands like Nivea, Bank of America, Volvo Group, Absolut Vodka, Air Asia and Pepsi.

Foap is free and will not only pay you a $5 license fee for the pictures you take, but will also give you 50% of the commission every time you sell a photo. Foap also offers easy payouts thanks to PayPal integration.

But that's not all. You can also sell photos taken with your cellphone — or digital camera — on other stock photo sites such as Getty Images, Shutterstock, iStock, Adobe Stock, and potentially earn even more.

For example, Getty Images will price a high-resolution photo in its online catalogue for as high as $575 — and pay you a 20% commission if it's sold. In this case, that's about $143 for a single photo each time it's downloaded!

More often, however, Getty Images will charge its premium access (frequent) customers much less, so your earnings on a download might be as low as a few bucks. However, even if your photo is priced much lower, you can earn hundreds of dollars from its continuous use.

The only drawback to Getty Images is that it retains exclusive rights to your photos, whereas other sites such iStock (which is owned by Getty Images) allow you to sell your work to other agencies as well. Of course, most of these services have a lower base rate of around 15%, meaning you'll be paid significantly less for your photos if you choose to shop them around. However, iStock does offer an exclusivity option that pays you 25% by default and up to 45% depending on the amount of downloads.

And for more information on how you can become a paid photographer and earn additional income simply by using your smartphone, visit Foap.com, Shutterstock.com, iStockphoto.com, GettyImages.com and Stock.Adobe.com.